YOU CANNOT HOLD BACK THE DAWN

you cannot hold back the Dawn

faith and love in a new dimension

Rev. John C. Dowd

ST. PAUL EDITIONS

Nihil Obstat:
Rev. Msgr. John G. Hogan

Imprimatur:
✠ Humberto Cardinal Medeiros
Archbishop of Boston

February 6, 1974

Library of Congress Catalog Card Number 74–75619

Printed in U.S.A. by the Daughters of St. Paul
50 St. Paul's Ave., Boston, Ma. 02130

The Daughters of St. Paul are
an international religious congregation
serving the Church with the communications media.

Contents

Foreword

The title for our reflections is drawn from an anecdote found within these pages. It concerns an Easter-time visitor to Palestine who spent a fretful night waiting for the sunrise service to begin at our Lord's tomb. "Will the night never end?" he asked his guide.

"Never fear, my friend," the Christian Arab replied. "The day will come. You cannot hold back the dawn."

These shared reflections cover many topics, many aspects of life, many spiritual truths, many experiences. But one theme pervades them all, a theme of joyous optimism:

"Storms and trials darken everyone's life. But the dawn always comes. It came for Christ and His followers. It has come repeatedly for His Church. And if we but wait patiently and trustfully, it will come for each one of us."

"I consider it a sign of great mercy shown me
by the Lord Jesus that He continues
to give me His peace,
and even external signs of grace.
I am told that these explain
the imperturbable serenity which allows me
to enjoy, in every hour of my day,
a simplicity and meekness of soul
that keep me ready to leave everything
at a moment's notice and depart for life eternal."

—POPE JOHN XXIII

In Search of Peace

Dante, the great Italian poet, was once asked what he sought most in life and he replied: "I am searching for that which everyone seeks—peace and rest." This is the petition we make for our dead: May they rest in peace. But can't we expect some measure of peace in this present life? We shall always remember that peace was our Lord's special legacy to us:

"'Peace' is my farewell to you,
my peace is my gift to you;
I do not give it to you as the world gives peace"
(Jn. 14:27).

By and large, the world has had only few and brief periods of peace, and even in those intervals, peace has always been rather precarious. Peace was almost unknown in the time of Christ. There was the great "Pax Romana," but it was a sullen peace maintained by force.

Six hundred years earlier, a pagan temple had been built to Janus, the god of beginnings, after whom our month of January is named. It was decreed that the gates of this temple should always be open in times of peace and closed in times of war. But only for three short periods in those six hundred years had the temple gates been open. It was a world that hungered for peace.

The world of today longs more than ever for peace. Every normal person wants peace. There is something radically wrong with persistent trouble-makers, those unhappy people who resent others' being happy. The desire for peace is deeply rooted and universal. We like nature best in its peaceful moods—the still beauty of a moonlit night, the placid surface of a lake and the serenity of a summer's day. We admire those who remain calm in disturbed situations; we are comforted by peaceful thoughts, soothed by soft music and cheered by the company of peace-loving people.

Our Lord spoke often about peace—the word is mentioned in the Gospels nearly a hundred times. One of the most popular prophecies concerning the Messiah was that He would bring peace to mankind. He was to be the Prince of peacemakers; His reign of peace would have no end. Angels heralded His coming with a glad message of peace.

St. Paul invariably begins and often ends his letters with the prayer that those to whom he is writing may have peace. With us, peace can have a rather negative meaning because it implies scarcely anything more than freedom from war or trouble. For a Jew, however, the word peace had a more positive and extensive meaning. The Hebrew word is "Shalom" and it is used as a greeting and means not just the absence of disturbance, but perfect well-being, happiness and friendship.

Christ used the word frequently, and He instructed His disciples to bless with peace the homes where they were welcomed: "Peace to this house" (Lk. 10:5). We should be comforted by this because it reminds us that God wants us to have well-being and happiness in our everyday lives. Whenever He comes to us, whether in joy or in sorrow, He always greets us with the kindly word "Shalom." He wanted the whole Jewish nation to have peace. "If only you had known the path to peace this day; but you have completely lost it from view!" (Lk. 19:42) It grieved Him deeply that His offer was rejected; He desired peace for them so ardently. He desires each one of us to have peace in our hearts and homes. We, too, yearn for it. How can we obtain it?

Since peace is a blessing and a grace of God, we must pray that it may be given us. In every Mass the Church makes us do this, especially just before receiving Holy Communion, so that we might have the proper dispositions for our Lord's "Shalom." We should also pray for peace in times of stress and temptation when we tend to become agitated and even to panic. We think of the sudden storm on the Lake of Galilee and Christ averting the danger: "The wind fell off and everything grew calm" (Mk. 4:39). The very fact of praying for peace can have a steadying, pacifying effect upon one.

We usually associate quietness with peace—we sometimes say, "peace and quiet," coupling the two together. This is quite natural because terror comes to us first through the ear—sudden strange sounds at night such as footsteps in an empty house, the screams of a maniac and the ferocious snarls of wild animals. One of the earliest fears of a child is said to be the fear of loud noises. A demonstration ceases to be peaceful as soon as the raucous chanting and the angry shouting begin. Perhaps this is one reason why very deaf people are often placid.

We need the occasional quiet of solitude if we are to have peace. Certain hidden springs of our being are tapped when we are alone. The artist, the writer, the musician and the creative worker must be alone to concentrate on the thoughts they wish to express. But there are times when we all feel the need for peace and quietness. A child will sometimes hide under a table or seek a secluded corner of the garden to play alone in its magic world of imagination.

Even the Son of God seems to have had this desire because often He would steal away at night to some solitary spot and seek the peace of prayerful communion with His Father. Sometimes, too, He would take His apostles away from the crowds for rest in some quiet place.

Years ago, the poet Wordsworth wrote, "The world is too much with us." Nowadays, radio and television bring the world into our very homes. Our disturbed age of strife and violence is the noisiest and most talkative age in history. "They cry 'peace, peace,' but there is no peace." Talk and discussion are considered to be the sole means of solving all our problems.

Communications are of course necessary. We are social beings; we depend upon one another and are made to live together, but we are also made to live with God. There must be regular times when we seek Him in quiet reflection and prayer. We can be certain of peace in His presence. He says to us, "It is I. Do not be afraid!" (Mt. 14:27) He counsels us to be at peace and know that He is God.

However, it would be a mistake to think that peace means only solitude and quiet. Most of us dream of getting away from the hustle and bustle, and of living "far from the madding crowd's ignoble strife." But how many of us are able to do this? And even if we could, can we be sure of having peace? We might see a little house in some secluded retreat and no sooner do we exclaim, "Here surely there is peace!" than a careworn face appears at a window and looks at us with troubled eyes. Wherever we go, we always take with us a potential disturber of peace—our own self.

Peace is not escapism. "Do not suppose that my mission on earth is to spread peace," Christ said. "My mission is to spread, not peace, but division" (Mt. 10:34). What did He mean? Simply that we cannot have peace at any price. A kind of warfare is necessary: a warfare against self. Emerson said, "Nothing can bring you peace but yourself." Peace needs to be within us, in our mind and conscience. We cannot have peace if we harbor thoughts of pride, hatred, anger, resentment and discontent. "Your attitude must be that of Christ," exhorts St. Paul (Phil. 2:5). We shall have Christ's peace if we have His way of thinking about people and events. And we must make our peace with Him; we must remove all guilt from our conscience.

Peace is defined as "the tranquillity of order." Peace does not just happen by chance. Order is one of its chief elements. It is true there is much disorder in the natural world. There are cruel and seemingly purposeless happenings that affect even the innocent: death and disease, earthquakes and hurricanes, floods and famines. Our earth is a disaster-prone area.

Nevertheless, human reason and our Christian Faith alike tell us that order always prevails and rules not only our tiny earth but the mighty universe about us. Einstein said, "I cannot believe that God plays dice with the cosmos." "We know," says St. Paul, "that God makes all things work together for the good of those who have been called according to his decree" (Rom. 8:28). We are not the helpless victims of a cruel, capricious fate, but the children of a loving Father. The stronger our trust in God, the more stable will be our peace.

If peace is the tranquillity of order, then we should try to make our lives well ordered. Appointed as Apostolic Vicar to Bulgaria in 1925, Pope John said, "I insert in my coat of arms the words 'Obedience and peace' which Cesare Baronius used to say every day, when he kissed the Apostle's foot in St. Peter's. These words are in a way my own history and my life."

The right order of creatures is obedience and submission to the Creator's will. For this reason Christ teaches us to pray, "Your will be done on earth as it is in heaven" (Mt. 6:10). We can only experience peace when we have union with God. The angels over Bethlehem proclaimed peace on earth to men of good will. We have good will if our wills are one with the will of God who is the source of all goodness, happiness and peace. The troubled Dante came at last to realize this because he wrote those lovely words, "In His will is our peace."

It is not selfish to desire peace. Spiritual writers tell us that peace is essential to every soul and that evil spirits seek by deceit and discouragement to destroy peace and consolation. St. Ignatius says that deep inward peace and joy are signs of a good will and spirit and they are not even incompatible with a life outwardly burdened with trials and suffering. Our Lord said:

> "Blest too the peacemakers, they shall be called sons of God" (Mt. 5:9).

He wants us to be more than just peaceable people. He wants us to do all we can to make peace among those with whom we live and with whom we come in contact. This will mean ridding ourselves of prejudices, overcoming our natural antipathies and having consideration for the opinions and rights of others.

We live in a divided world with its iron curtains, walls and barriers, its suspicions and hatreds. We must do what we can to remove all man-made obstacles. No one knew better than our Lord the tragedy of the fierce rivalries and jealousies that separate men and women from one another. Even His own chosen apostles argued among themselves about who should be the greatest.

Where there are people, there is always the possibility of strife and rancor, whether it is in the family, the parish or the neighborhood. There are those who are disruptive influences and those who reconcile and heal. We believe that we are God's children; we must endeavor to be His peacemakers. But first we must have peace in our own hearts. It is only then that we shall really desire, as did St. Francis of Assisi, that others might experience our joy.

"Lord, make me an instrument of Your peace. Where there is hatred, let me sow love; where there is doubt, faith; where there is injury, pardon; where there is despair, hope; where there is darkness, light; where there is sadness, joy."

Who Are the Happy People?

Many books have been written about happiness. Their titles and contents may differ, but they all have the same attractive aim—happiness. To mention just a few: *The Road to Happiness; The Search for Happiness; Happiness, Its Pursuit and Attainment; The Science of Happiness; The Secret of Happiness;* and *How To Be Happy and Make Others Happy.* That there is a demand for such books is a proof, if proof be needed, of the universal human desire for happiness and of the difficulty in finding it.

But why so much study and searching? Is happiness so very mysterious and elusive? The dictionary definition is simple enough: "Happiness is the conscious possession and enjoyment of good." Why then do we make such hard going of the search for happiness?

One reason is because we often confuse happiness with pleasure, which is a very different thing. Pleasure mostly comes through the senses and usually depends on external things such as comfort, money, food and clothes. You can have all these things and still not be happy. Happiness can be independent of them because it is within us; it is of the mind and spirit. Moreover, pleasure satiates; our appetites can have a surfeit of pleasure, but we can never have too much happiness.

Who are the happiest people? There is no simple answer unless it is that they are the ones who are too busy to notice whether or not they are happy. Are the happiest people those who have achieved some great success in life? Often their biographies reveal they were the prey of deep depression and that they were happiest when they were struggling after success.... "The struggle is the prize."

Alexander the Great is said to have wept in his tent because there were no more countries for him to conquer. Are young people happier than the elderly? Youth has its problems and we are not young for long. The unmarried are said to be more prone to suicide than the married, but divorce statistics are not reassuring.

On the whole, it almost seems that the happiest people are those fortunate enough to possess a naturally happy disposition, those who have an inborn vitality and zest for living. But at least we all have an inborn capacity to learn, and there are many who have succeeded in making their lives happy, regardless of their circumstances.

Here are what might be termed three main constituents of happiness:

First, life must have a meaning and a purpose if it is to be happy. It is significant that most of those who complain bitterly of the miseries of life are not the poor and afflicted, but those who have been smiled upon and favored. There was, for instance, the English poet, Lord Byron, who lived a life of pleasure, and yet he wrote: "The worm, the canker and the grief are mine alone." The French writer Voltaire had a life of comfort and was acclaimed by the public more than any other man of his time, but he made this comment on life: "The end of it is dreary, the middle is worthless and the commencement is ridiculous.... I wish I had never been born."

Talleyrand was brilliant and famous, and although he had always lived in luxury, on his eighty-third birthday he wrote: "Eighty-three years of my life are now passed, with no result but a great weariness, physical and moral, a profound sense of discouragement with regard to the future and disgust for the past."

Why were these men so bitter and disillusioned about life? Simply because they had lost sight of its true purpose. What is purposeless is useless. It is difficult for anyone to have any interest in a task which has no purpose.

Supposing a group of men are supplied with tools, bricks and mortar, but they are not given any plans or architectural designs, and moreover, they are told that the structure they build will be pulled down and destroyed in a few months or years. We would not be surprised if these men found no joy in their work and rejected it as senseless and crazy.

Without a belief in an after-life, this present life is purposeless; it is, in the words of Shakespeare, "a tale told by an idiot, full of sound and fury and signifying nothing." One of the main reasons why so many people are bored with life and find it stale and unprofitable, is because for them life lacks a spiritual purpose, a purpose outside and above purely material satisfactions and bodily pleasures. "What profit does a man show who gains the whole world and destroys himself in the process?" Christ has said (Mk. 8:36). He also said,

"I came
that they might have life
and have it to the full" (Jn. 10:10).

Even though this life is a time of toiling and sowing, to the Christian it is a joyous, challenging time because it has a meaning and a purpose.

Contentment is another ingredient of happiness, especially contentment with the small, simple things of life. A political prisoner once remarked that his dreadful experience had given him a feeling of appreciation for the ordinary things of life which most people take for granted: the ability to live with one's family, to talk with one's friends and to breathe fresh air. When deprived of these things, we suddenly realize how important they are.

"Always to be happy," said Bishop Keppler, "is an art, and not a very difficult one. It consists merely in training oneself to perceive, appreciate and thankfully utilize little joys."

Contentment means taking the rough with the smooth in life and seeing the silver lining in every cloud, the prospective good in some present evil. Christ spoke of His future sufferings, but He also predicted His resurrection. St. Paul said, "I consider the sufferings of the present to be as nothing compared with the glory to be revealed in us" (Rom. 8:18). He and Silas sang in their prison.

St. Thomas More, waiting death in the Tower of London, said that his enemies, by their persecution of him, had done him a great favor.

A philosophical detachment can be an aid to contentment, and a sense of humor is invaluable, even if sometimes it is wry and whimsical. A worried gardener wrote to a government department: "I have tried everything in your booklet on how to get rid of dandelions, but I've still got them." The department replied: "If you have carried out all our instructions and you still have dandelions, there is only one thing left for you to do—learn to love dandelions." There are many varieties of dandelions and often we have no alternative but to accept them.

Being sorry for oneself is fatal to happiness. A lady signing herself "Arlene" wrote to the sagacious Pauline Phillips, better known perhaps as "Dear Abby":

"My husband has always been very close to his mother and she has never cared much for me. I asked my husband if I were drowning and his mother were drowning, which one would he save. He said, 'My mother, because I owe her more.' I'm terribly hurt, Abby, what shall I do?"

Abby replied briefly: "Dear Arlene, learn to swim."

This advice is similar to what the White Queen gave to Alice: "Consider what a girl you are. Consider what a long way you have come. Consider what o'clock it is. Consider anything, only don't cry." Self-pity is self-destroying.

Boredom is an enemy of happiness. Lindbergh complained of it repeatedly, even on his historic flight over the Atlantic. Bertrand Russell wrote, "Half the sins of mankind are caused by fear of boredom." Erich Fromm calls it "the illness of the age" and claims it is the root-cause of violence and drug addiction. "Most of my patients come to me," said Dr. H. Ward, "simply because they are bored." The British actor, George Sanders, left a note citing boredom as a reason for his suicide.

To be happy, we must surround ourselves with many interests. Withdrawal is the main characteristic of boredom. A person no longer is interested in anything. His receiver is off the hook.

Selfishness destroys happiness. It produces envy, suspicion, greed and a discontented, complaining attitude. On the other hand, an unselfish concern and care for others is always rewarding. As someone put it, "Some cause happiness where they go, but others, when they go."

Happiness is elusive; it has been described as a by-product of life. If you set out seeking it for yourself, you will be disappointed because it is only found by those who are trying to find it for others.

Finally, the last and perhaps the most important requirement for happiness is love. Centuries ago, the great and learned St. Augustine gave this definition of happiness: "Happiness consists in loving and in being loved." These are two deeply-rooted human needs.

In 1971, it was estimated there were more than eleven million Americans living alone. Said Mrs. Jay Winter, secretary of the National Association of the Pet Industry, "There are millions of lonely single people in this country who want to come home to something more than a bare apartment. They want something to fondle and love, and a cat or a dog help fulfill that need."

How many lives are tragic failures because they are empty, loveless lives! We feel that we are somebody when someone loves us. A child may have been neglected or cruelly treated and it is sullen and suspicious, but let someone—a teacher or friend—show sympathy and love, and the child's nature changes. "Perfect love casts out all fear" (1 Jn. 4:18).

The Christian knows who is the happiest Person in all history. He is no other than the One who is perfect love, love incarnate, Christ, the Man of Sorrows, but also the joyous Son of God—perfectly loved of His Father. He is the "beloved Son" (Mk. 1:11) who loved His Father and all mankind perfectly. His message to our sad world is called "the good news." And so indeed it is, for God Himself is telling us that He knows, cherishes and loves each one of us.

Someone has said, "When you watch religion at work, you find a morality; when you converse with religion in its thoughtful moods, you find a theology; but when you get to the heart of religion, you find a song...." Christianity began with songs of rejoicing. There was the Magnificat of our Lady, the Benedictus of Zechariah and the Glorias of the angel host at Bethlehem. What better way of rejoicing and praising could there be than singing? Christ's coming on earth was something to set mankind singing until the end of time.

St. John Vianney used to say, "It is always springtime in the heart that loves God." The French have a saying, "A sad saint is a sad sort of a saint." There should always be a song in our hearts. When there isn't, it means that we have forgotten the gladsome tidings.

> "...and he who loves me will be loved by my Father" (Jn. 14:21).
>
> "All this I tell you
> that my joy may be yours
> and your joy may be complete" (Jn. 15:11).
>
> "...your hearts will rejoice
> with a joy no one can take from you" (Jn. 16:22).

Books about happiness will continue to be written, and men and women will never cease to seek it, but in the end the search for happiness is no other than the search for God. Only the possession and enjoyment of God, the supreme goodness, can satisfy human aspirations and desires. St. Augustine knew this from his own bitter experience: "You have made us for Yourself, O Lord, and our hearts are restless until they rest in You."

Seeking God

The philosopher Nietzche uttered words that were as despairing as they were blasphemous, and perhaps the best commentary on them was that scrawled on a wall in a town in Europe. Someone had written defiantly,

"God is dead."
–Nietzche

Underneath, someone else had added,
"Nietzche is dead."
–God

It is not so surprising that God should seem dead or non-existent to some in the world of today, since it is an era of great scientific and technological progress, a time of many human achievements. In consequence, God may seem hidden and unreal.

However, the problem is as old as humanity. Job said,

"Oh, that today I might find him....
But if I go to the east, he is not there;
or to the west, I cannot perceive him;
...he is veiled, and I see him not" (Jb. 23:3, 8, 9).

Even the great visionary Isaiah complained that God often hid Himself.

This cosmic age of gigantic human achievements is also a time of bewilderment and fear. The hoped-for blessings of a scientific epoch have not materialized. Instead, mankind is confronted with new and bigger problems; security and stability are lacking and there are gloomy forebodings of approaching disasters. Humanity's need of God is greater than ever, and yet God seems hidden. It cannot be that He has ceased to care for His creatures, but we share the yearning of the psalmist of old:

"How long, O Lord? Will you utterly forget me?
How long will you hide your face from me?"
(Ps. 13:2)

But does God hide Himself from us? We insult Him if we picture Him as childishly tantalizing us, deliberately concealing His presence. On the contrary, by the very nature of things, He must reveal Himself. Our reason tells us not only that God exists, but that He is a Person who loves, and love must disclose itself. God has revealed Himself and continues to do so, in very many wonderful and different ways.

He has revealed Himself in His creation, which mirrors His infinite power and wisdom. Science has not created the wonders of the universe, but merely discovered and cleverly used some of what already existed. The telescope and the microscope alike have uncovered many of the marvels of God's creation. Someone has pointed out that even flowers are a strong proof of God's existence: strictly speaking, they are not really necessary, yet they exist in all their perfection of color, scent and variety. They are a reflection of God's beauty and perfection. We take them for granted, but our Lord said, "Learn a lesson from the way the wild flowers grow" (Mt. 6:28).

There is also moral beauty—such things as goodness, heroism and self-sacrifice. God reveals Himself in the human conscience. We were born knowing that kindness is better than cruelty, the truth better than a lie, love better than hate. Where did these certainties come from? Thought and will, the powers to communicate and love are some of the elements of human personality, and they must have come from an even greater Personality whom we call God.

God reveals Himself to us in the Scriptures. "Search the Scriptures...," Christ said (Jn. 5:39). The Bible is the word of God. It is a collection of historical documents, but its ancient teachings are fresh and vital. "O beauty ever ancient, ever new!" said St. Augustine. The Scripture scholar, Fr. A. Jones, figured he must have read the Gospels more than four thousand times. Yet he said, "Each time I read them, I see something new."

God has revealed Himself through His Son. "In times past," says St. Paul, "God spoke in fragmentary and varied ways to our fathers through the prophets; in this, the final age he has spoken to us through his Son" (Heb. 1:1). People have wondered what God is like, almost blindly groping their way towards Him and often forming wrong opinions about Him. But our Lord gives us certain knowledge of God. "Whoever has seen me has seen the Father" (Jn. 14:9).

Finally, God reveals Himself in the teaching of His Church. The Church was not the idea or invention of the disciples—"Let's get together and start a community." The Church was deliberately and for a set purpose instituted by Christ. He meant it to be a continuation of His coming on earth, a perpetuation of His saving work until the end of time. He looked upon it as His very own and He founded it with His divine power on the firm rock of authority. He solemnly declared,

"As the Father has sent me,
so I send you" (Jn. 20:21).

"...go, therefore and make disciples of all the nations" (Mt. 28:19).

"He who hears you, hears me" (Lk. 10:16).

"And know that I am with you always..." (Mt. 28:20).

Although it is not true to say that God hides Himself from us, nevertheless it must be admitted that God's presence is, to a very great extent, mysterious and concealed. His very nature makes it so. "*Deus cognitus, Deus nullus* – a known God is no God at all."

Above the entrance to a museum someone had carved in the stone a text from the book of Job:

"Lo, these are but the outlines of his ways,
and how faint is the word we hear!" (Jb. 26:14)

None of us can claim to know God fully; He is so much more than any part of His creation and we only get glimpses of Him.

A tiny insect crawling up the wall of a vast cathedral knows nothing about the beauty or the purpose of the building or of the life that goes on around it. We who are isolated on this little speck of floating dust that we call earth can only dimly perceive the presence and nature of God the Creator, the supreme Spirit, the Being who is infinite in all His perfections. The human mind is only able to absorb morsels of the natural sciences and still less of the knowledge about God.

But we suffer a further limitation when it is a matter of knowing the spiritual and supernatural. Just as darkness is caused by the earth turning from the sun, so when we turn away from God, we enter the shadows. Sin and self-seeking darken the mind.

"Blest are the single-hearted
for they shall see God" (Mt. 5:8).

A great musician said that he dared not listen to poor music because it spoiled his ear for listening to the best music. The state of a person's mind can make a difference to what he sees. Where we would just see a tangled growth of weeds and wildflowers, an artist would see beauty and a botanist would recognize each by name and perhaps discover something rare. To the pure, all things are pure, but a depraved person sees something to sneer at in everything.

It is the same with us and God. We either blind ourselves to Him, or if we are pure in heart, pure in our motives, wholehearted in our love of Him, we shall see His goodness, His love and His presence everywhere.

Although God may not hide Himself from us, nevertheless, He does not force Himself upon us. He respects our freedom and asks us to come to Him, even to seek Him. "Seek first his kingship over you... (Mt. 6:33). "Seek, and you will find" (Mt. 7:7). In the Greek words of this passage, persistence is implied. We must keep on seeking.

Here then is another reason why God may seem so hidden—perhaps we only seek Him halfheartedly or not at all. Christ said, "Blest are they who hunger and thirst for holiness..." (Mt. 5:6). We must hunger and thirst for God.

Patience and persistence are essential in every sphere of life. You cannot master a language or achieve success in athletics except by months, even years, of study and training. It is said of Rachmaninoff that after a long recital he would sit at his piano going over and over some passage that had not satisfied him.

If we are indifferent and self-satisfied, God will be hidden from us. Christ tells us we must be like the man finding a treasure that was hidden in a field and selling everything he has to buy the field. Many people fail to persevere in their quest for God simply because they do not sufficiently desire Him and are not prepared to make every effort and sacrifice to possess Him.

Pastor Neimoller tells a true story about an incident during the Russian occupation of Romania. Two armed soldiers entered a church with guns in their hands. There were a number of people sheltered in the church and the Russians instructed them: "Those who do not abandon the Christian Faith will be shot at once. Those who are willing to give up their Faith, move over to the right." Some walked over to the right and were ordered to leave the church and go home. They fled for their lives. The soldiers lowered their guns when they were alone with the small group of remaining Christians; they embraced them and said, "We, too, are Christians, but we wanted to know those who consider the Faith worth dying for and whom we could trust."

The Christian life is demanding. It is not just for those who are mildly interested. The Christian does not say, "I am curious and interested in Christ." He says, "For me, to live is Christ" (cf. Phil. 1:21). Very often it is only when we are suffering that we realize our helplessness, and experiencing a desperate need for God, seek Him at last in earnest. Peguy said, "Christendom will come back in the hour of distress."

We live in a time of radical changes, a time of doubts and questioning and a time when many are abandoning their Faith. It is a time to search for the truth about life, about our destiny, about ourselves, but above all, about our God.

Man the Mysterious

A young girl was rather late returning home from a dance. Stern and self-righteous, her father greeted her, "Hello, daughter of Satan!" Of course he asked for it, and meekly the girl responded, "Hello, Father."

Yes, there is something of Satan in us all at times. Christ said to Peter once, "Get out of my sight, you satan!" (Mt. 16:23); and St. John says of Judas that "...Satan entered his heart" (Jn. 13:27).

Human beings are very puzzling. They are so unpredictable. We can be full of admiration for their achievements—they are capable of great heroism and self-sacrifice; they are industrious and inventive; they have built cathedrals, composed symphonies and poems. With Hamlet we exclaim in wonderment, "What a piece of work is man! How noble in reason! How infinite in faculty...in action how like an angel; in apprehension how like a god!"

But there are other times when we are ashamed and disgusted by the depravity of men and women. We see them cruel, unjust, perverse—destroying the very things they have prized and loved; arrogant yet foolish, slaves to animal greed and lust. We wonder at God's patience and exclaim with the psalmist,

"O Lord...
What is man that you should be mindful of him?" (Ps. 8:5)

Because of this unpredictable behavior, people tend to be divided in their judgment of the human race. Some are pessimistic and say that human nature is hopelessly evil; men and women are just clever animals. Other people are optimists and declare that human nature is fundamentally good and that we are slowly but surely evolving to greater perfection.

The Christian attitude is neither pessimistic nor optimistic, but realistic. We believe that God made human beings different from any other creature on earth—in His own likeness. They have understanding and a free will; therefore they have a capacity for goodness, truth and beauty far surpassing that of all the other creatures around them. But this capacity has been injured, it has become distorted by evil. We are indeed created by God to be His children, but we have become prodigals; God's original intention and plan for us has been seriously interfered with; the wound to our nature was self-inflicted.

The doctrine of the Fall affects each one of us. It is based upon what the Bible and the centuries-old teaching of the Church tell us, and it also corresponds all too well with what we see in ourselves. It is a description of you and me, for we know good and evil, yet we often stifle our conscience, we yield to temptation, we choose to do evil and we try to blame others.

The doctrine of the Fall is not gloomy and pessimistic. The story in the Bible has a happy ending, because it has hope and promise in it. To be fallen is not a hopeless condition; it implies the possibility of getting up again.

As an illustration of this: suppose while out walking one day, you see a deep hole in the ground and in it a little dog. It is injured, frightened, and unable to get out. You climb into the hole to rescue the struggling dog. There are other slimy creatures in the mud and darkness of the hole, but you don't bother to get them out. They belong there. The little dog, on the contrary, is out of its element. When we say that man has fallen, we mean he does not belong to the evil into which he has fallen. He can be rescued, or to use a great Biblical word, "saved."

The history of the people of Israel might be summed up in the words: "hope of salvation." The promise made to the human race was kept alive by their prophets:

"Rejoice heartily...O daughter Jerusalem!
...your king shall come to you;
a just savior is he..." (Zec. 9:9).
"I will put salvation within Zion,
and give to Israel my glory" (Is. 46:13).
"In his days Judah shall be saved,
Israel shall dwell in security" (Jer. 23:6).

But this hope was not confined to the Israelites. In the Eastern Mediterranean countries immediately preceding the birth of Christ, innumerable engraved stones bear a word which expresses the aspirations of the cultivated world at that time. The word is "soteria"—salvation. People wanted desperately that mysterious thing, salvation, and they were sure it would come through a religious rite.

Christ is the Savior of mankind. "The Son of Man has come to search out and save what was lost," He said (Lk. 19:10). It had been predicted of him: "He will save his people from their sins" (Mt. 1:21). Mary was overjoyed:

"My being proclaims the greatness of the Lord,
my spirit finds joy in God my savior..." (Lk. 1:46-47).

Simeon gave thanks: "For my eyes have witnessed your saving deed..." (Lk. 2:30). Only Christ can save.

Plymouth, England, is a naval base, and some years ago during "Navy Week" celebrations there, the festivities were spoiled by a distressing accident. A young sailor was demonstrating a new life-saving apparatus. But something went wrong and he lost his life. The irony of it! The life-saving apparatus was the cause of his death. Spiritual quacks are like that. They claim to be able to save, but only Christ can save.

It was widely thought once that science was the cure for all our ills. Instead of "The Bible says," or, "The Church says," people said, "Science says." Now people are beginning to think otherwise. Science seems more bent on the destruction than the salvation of humanity. Science cannot tell us the meaning and purpose of life. In this scientific age there is more emotional illness, more cruelty, violence and vandalism than ever before.

Man cannot live by bread alone—not even when it is scientifically baked.

Christ still saves. His redemption is applied to us in the Mass and the sacraments. In every Mass His saving sacrifice is continued. In the sacrament of Penance He pardons and heals. In Holy Communion He nourishes, strengthens, and is the pledge of our eternal salvation. He still comes to seek and to save that which is lost. Sinners are of infinite value in His eyes. He is under no illusions about us; He knows what is in man, yet He bids us to be perfect, even as our Father in heaven is perfect.

The Truth About Ourselves

A journalist once interviewed Rudolph Valentino, the one-time movie idol. Dress and photographs of himself were the only things that interested the actor. Hundreds of his portraits were scattered about his room, and he eagerly discussed them with his interviewer. He had no other interests, no opinion on acting or on the film as a medium of art.

Sir Thomas Lipton, the Scot who started life in a factory earning a pittance of a wage and who became a wealthy chain-store owner, also collected photographs. They were of royalty and himself. He boasted that no other commoner had ever entertained so many kings and queens as he, and his conversation was full of such expressions as "Her Majesty told me...," "The Kaiser once said to me...," "The Prince of Wales and I...."

We smile at such patent pride and vanity. Pride is often spoken of as "foolish" and so indeed it is, but pride is no trivial matter. It is deadly. We recall Christ's words, "I watched Satan fall from the sky like lightning" (Lk. 10:18). Shakespeare said, "By that sin fell the angels." Man, too, fell through pride; his first experience of temptation was to pride: "...you will be like gods..." (Gn. 3:5).

Pride is the basic sin; it is the root of the enmities and crimes, the griefs and miseries that form the sad human scene; it is the "dark tuberculosis of the human spirit."

Pride is therefore in all of us. It may not always be visible to us. One of the insidious characteristics of pride is that while it is easy to see in others, it is difficult to detect in ourselves. Yet if anyone should dare to correct or contradict us, disregard or slander us, we are outraged and indignant. We find it difficult to acknowledge a fault or a mistake, and it hurts us to have to make an apology. Our pride reveals itself in numerous little ways.

The remedy for the disease is humility. But what is humility? It is something rare and elusive. "Humility is a virtue all preach, and none practice." Of course we all think we are humble, but this is a bad sign. "When you know you've got it, you've lost it." Humility is not a pretense—calling ourselves worms and miserable sinners. We are human beings and not worms; we are sinners, but we are not miserable in the sense that we have no hope of forgiveness or conversion.

"Humility is the truth," said St. Teresa, and the truth about us is that we are not gods, we are only creatures. We are not independent, all-knowing and all-powerful. In fact, the truth is often even worse, because we are potentially selfish and foolish, cruel and inhuman.

Spiritual writers always stress the importance of humility, telling us that it is the basis of every virtue. But none of us is born humble; we have to acquire humility, to learn about it and then to practice it. None of this comes easily. Humility does not attract us; it seems a weakness. It will help us, therefore, if we consider some of the advantages humility always brings. This lowly virtue can be a great asset.

Humility produces peace of mind. "True humility is contentment." "Humble hearts have humble desires." Those who are humble escape from the pressures of the over-ambitious and the seekers after the limelight. Humble people commit themselves to God with all the confidence little children have in their parents. He who is humble will ever have God as his guide.

Humility helps us to be patient. Impatience might seem to be a small fault, but it can cause unpleasantness and it may be the symptom of a deeply-rooted pride. We get impatient because we do not get our own way or because others disagree with us. Humility makes us aware of our limitations and faults; it helps us to be tolerant of others, respecting their opinions and wishes, and bearing with their weaknesses.

Seeing a drunkard in the street, St. Philip Neri said, "There, but for the grace of God, goes Philip."

Humility teaches us unselfishness. The proud are self-conscious, aware of their dignity and learning, jealously guarding rights and privileges. And how many good causes have been abandoned because someone was offended, was not consulted, or refused to overlook some unintentional slight! How often we have forgotten the Scriptural counsel of perfection, "When a person strikes you on the right cheek, turn and offer him the other" (Mt. 5:39). The saints are utterly unselfish because they are humble.

Begging money for his orphanage, St. Clement Hofbauer entered a beer hall, and the proprietor shouted, "Get out of here, priest!" He then spat in his face. Clement was a big man and was known to have had a fiery temper, but he calmly wiped his face and said, "That was for me. Now how about something for my orphanage?"

Humility brings us learning and wisdom. We have all met the person who knows everything, who is prejudiced, self-opinionated and cannot be taught anything. Einstein, for all his great genius, was said to have been always prepared to learn, even from childhood.

Sir Isaac Newton, the wisest man of his century, said, "I seem to have been only a boy playing on the seashore, now and then finding a smoother pebble or a prettier shell than usual, while the great ocean of truth lay all undiscovered before me." Great men have always been humble.

One winter's day a Cardinal was walking along a street in Rome and saw a bent old man slowly trudging along. "Old man," he said, "you should not be out in such weather. Where are you going?" Then he recognized Michelangelo, the greatest of the sculptors. "I am going to the School of Architecture," Michelangelo replied. "There is so much to learn and the time is so short."

It is pride that blinds many to belief in God, just as it was pride that caused the Pharisees to reject Christ—racial and nationalistic pride and pride in their knowledge of the Mosaic Law.

Humility makes prayer easier and more beneficial. Proud people never pray, or if they do, they pray as did the Pharisee in our Lord's story of the two men praying in the temple. The Pharisee was complacent and self-satisfied. He did not need anything, he had no sins to be forgiven; he did not require strength to overcome temptation, nor did he need to know more about God and His ways. He may have been a basically good man, but he was proud in spirit and his prayer went unrewarded. "How blest are the poor in spirit..."(Mt. 5:3). The humble person does not make the mistake of comparing himself with his fellow men, but with God, and he is deeply conscious of his sinfulness and need.

But even were there no advantages from humility, the Christian should want to be humble for no other reason than to be more Christlike. "...learn from me, for I am gentle and humble of heart" (Mt. 11:29). Our Lord's entire life was steeped in humiliations and He is constantly teaching us the hard lesson of humility.

St. Paul declares that in becoming man, Christ emptied Himself. He began His life on earth in utter obscurity and poverty. Although divine, He never sought any privileges, not even exemption from the hidden years of monotonous toil. He shunned all publicity, avoided the great centers of civilization and chose poor men as His companions. He wanted no acknowledgement for His great miracles and hid Himself when the people tried to make Him their earthly leader and king.

Humiliation marked the closing hours of His ministry. He washed the feet of His apostles, and then gave Himself as their spiritual food under the appearance of bread and wine. He was sold for a few pieces of silver, denied by His leading apostle and delivered over to an alien power that was hated by His nation.

His trial was a mockery. He was treated as a fool, ridiculed and spat upon. He who had had a pauper's birth died a criminal's death. He touched the lowest depths of degradation because He seemed even to have been abandoned by His Father.

"But I am a worm, not a man;
the scorn of men, despised by the people.

All who see me scoff at me;
they mock me with parted lips, they wag their heads:
'He relied on the Lord; let him deliver him,
let him rescue him, if he loves him'" (Ps. 22:7-9).

But no delivery came, because, as St. Paul says,
"...he humbled himself,
obediently accepting even death,
death on a cross!" (Phil. 2:8)

The Savior of mankind leads us along the way we must all take—the way back to God, the way of humble recognition of what we are, the way of humility. Other ways may be novel, more attractive and easier, but they are the dangerous ways of those who are crazed by delusions of grandeur.

The Riddle of Life

Everything nowadays is questioned, but there is a question that is as old as humanity. It was asked thousands of years ago by Hebrews, Greeks and Romans, and it is still being asked: "What is life? Why am I here?"

Life is certainly a perplexing problem. Poets and philosophers comment on its shortness. "Life is a night's encampment in the desert"; "a little gleam of time between two eternities"; "a bird's flight through the air." It is short because there is scarcely time for us to do all that lies in us, or to use all the God-given powers we possess, especially since death often comes prematurely. And it is short when you consider that a third of our lives is spent in sleep. Moreover, so much time is taken up with material cares and trivial occupations that little is left to live life in its fullest sense.

Then there are the countless anomalies and contradictions of life. Why are some crushed under one trouble after another, while others seem to escape lightly? Why is this child born blind or in terrible poverty? Virtue often goes unrewarded and vice prospers. And even when we get some happiness in life, either it is short-lived or it fails to come up to our expectations. "Life's enchanted cup but sparkles at the brim."

To one, life is sweet and he clings to it; another longs for the end and it will not come.

The anomalies are endless. Life is an enigma and the solution of such an intricate puzzle cannot be found in life itself. A story Fulton Ousler tells illustrates this fact:

In the rural area where he once lived, a mysterious man used to call the local telephone operator just before noon each day to inquire the exact time. Eventually the operator became curious. "Mister, would you mind telling me why you call like this every day?"

"Oh yes," was the answer, "I am the man who blows the town whistle at noon every day."

"Well, that's funny," replied the operator, "that really is funny, because every day I set our clock by your whistle."

Ousler ends his story with the comment that in spite of modern precision instruments, time is still calculated by the oldest of methods—from the observation of the sun and the planets outside our own earth.

We need to be told by an outside authority what life is all about. And God, the Creator of life, has told us. In the Scriptures, life is described as a journey or pilgrimage. Literally, this is how it was for God's people journeying through the desert wilderness. The much-traveled St. Paul says, "We know that while we dwell in the body we are away from the Lord" (2 Cor. 5:6). St. Peter, nearing the end of his own life's pilgrimage uses the phrase, "strangers and in exile" (1 Pt. 2:11), which is an echo of the aged and weary David:

"For I am but a wayfarer before you,
a pilgrim like all my fathers" (Ps. 39:13).
"My days are like a lengthening shadow,
and I wither like grass" (Ps. 102:12).

The Mass is using the language of the Scriptures when it speaks of the "pilgrim Church on earth."

Life is a journey. We set out in childhood and youth with zest and vigor; we paint the future in radiant hues; happiness is assured somewhere ahead. Then comes middle age, in some ways perhaps the most testing part of the journey. Our step is losing its spring; friends have come and gone; pain, failure and disillusionment have been encountered. True, there have been pleasant places and periods and we would have liked to linger, but we are on a journey and all is transitory. In old age we are nearing our journey's end and now at last there can be no more illusions; the rest and peace, the permanent and unalloyed happiness we crave lie only beyond the horizon of this world.

Life is a journey. Christ spent His earthly life in journeying, and each journey He took has a depth of meaning. He was born on a journey, and following close on His birth was the journey as a refugee into Egypt. As a child He was lost on a journey. Later, there was the journeying through the towns and villages of Palestine. Then came the triumphal journey into Jerusalem and afterwards the slow, agonizing journey to Calvary. Finally, there were the journeys to Emmaus, Galilee and to heaven.

Life is a journey. To some it appears to be a meaningless journey, but to us it is a journey from God who set our feet upon the road, and to God who awaits us at the end of the journey. We have here no abiding city. Our life's journey is through an alien land, not a homeland.

To view life as a journey or pilgrimage explains something, at least, of the meaning of life. It helps to explain the anomalies and the heartbreaks. At the end of the journey everything will be rectified and there will be happy reunions for all. We are travelers, and so we will be prepared for hardships. Yet we will start each new day with the confidence that all things work together for good to those who love God.

Everything is transitory, so we will remind ourselves, "I shall pass through this world but once. If, therefore, there is any kindness I can show, or any good I can do, let me do it now. Let me not defer or neglect it, for I shall not pass this way again."

And if sometimes we are in doubt of the way, or even lose it for a while, we shall know where to seek guidance. Like us, the apostles were often confused. They once said to Christ, "Lord...how can we know the way?"(Jn. 14:5) Jesus replied, "I am the way, and the truth and the life" (Jn. 14:6).

Because Christ is our way, our journey is holy, and because we journey through Him to the Father, we are not just travelers through life. Nor are we mere tourists. We are pilgrims. Our life is a pilgrimage. Were it otherwise, it would have no meaning or purpose.

Master of My Mind

An ingenious scientist has calculated that if the human brain were to be reproduced with mechanical components like those of a computer, it would cost a fortune to build, would require several million cubic feet of storage space, and would still lack the mental qualities of the human brain which is stored in a few inches of space.

The brain is indeed an intricate mechanism. Karl Stern, the famous neurologist, explains how in the simple act of moving one's little finger, a large set of the brain's millions of microscopically small cells is required. Each cell is like a miniature telephone exchange, receiving and transmitting messages. To describe their operations, one would have to write a book. Stern adds, "The normal and abnormal anatomy of the brain is so complicated and methods of investigation are so involved that most anatomists refrain from dealing with it."

It is this small, delicately-fashioned piece of mechanism which has given human beings their superiority over the rest of creation, produced masterpieces in the arts, philosophies and machines. But however wonderful the brain may be, it is no more than an instrument. It is not the whole, but only a part of you. Do you love with just your brain? Do you essentially live with only your brain?

The brain is your servant—a proof of this is that you can command your brain. We speak of "using" our brain. We can choose the things we want to think about; we can make our brain more efficient, overwork it, or neglect it altogether, so that it is undeveloped.

The real *you* is the soul—the soul which uses the brain. We think of it, in figurative language, as brooding over the brain cells and fissures like the Spirit of God over the face of the deep. Or again, we picture the soul playing upon the brain as upon an instrument, touching the keys so that thoughts and aspirations like music come from it—ideas that transcend time and space, reaching out to the infinite, to God Himself. The brain may suffer damage and, in consequence, not be able to function properly, but its owner will still be a human being and not just a vegetable. The soul is God's masterpiece of creation.

In giving us a brain, God has provided us with a remarkable piece of equipment to enable us to journey successfully through life. Indeed, the proper use of the brain might be said to be the whole art of living. Tapping his forehead, St. Philip Neri used to say, "Sanctity rests within the compass of a few inches."

The art of living simply means getting the best out of ourselves and life by training and using the brain so that we live as fully developed and responsible persons. It means keeping the peace, the whole peace and nothing but the peace with God and others. It means the avoidance of friction and therefore calls for a disciplined and controlled brain.

The brain is not in itself disciplined. It is, for example, easily distracted. No sooner have we begun to pray than our minds are off skipping and jumping about like grasshoppers. And the brain quickly forgets. We resolve to be patient or cheerful or kind, and then we are upset by someone or something and we become angry, or depressed, or selfish. On the other hand, the brain sometimes remembers too much.... We may be hurt or grieved or disappointed; perhaps nothing can be done about it, but the brain will keep on presenting the problem so that we have sleepless nights and we are difficult to live with.

But we must be fair. Is the brain really the culprit? After all, it is only a servant, an instrument. The fault lies with the owner and user of the brain, and only a bad workman blames his tools. Some people say they are not religious, they cannot believe in God, or prayer, or a life after death; but have they ever really taken the trouble to give serious consideration to these matters? Others say they cannot help having a bad temper or some other fault; or that they cannot help eating or drinking too much, or worrying, but are they just giving excuses instead of reasons?

Such people are like a man in a car who gets a flat tire and who keeps on driving, blaming the road or the steering, or the car, or even his passengers, and doing nothing about the real fault. They may be educated people, experts and specialists in different branches of knowledge, but they do not use their brains in all the areas of their lives. They allow feelings, prejudices and moods to rule them, and often they are just lazy and overindulgent. Emerson said, "Man holds an inward talk with himself alone which it behooves him to regulate well."

The art of living then, depends upon our using and being in control of our brain. "Peace rules the day, where reasons rule the mind." There are times in life when everything seems to go wrong. Yet although we may have little control over people and circumstances, we do have within us an apparatus which we can control and which can enable us to deal with any emergency. The mind is a sacred enclosure, a temple of the Holy Spirit, in which nothing harmful or disturbing can stay without our permission. "My mind a kingdom is."

We can say to ourselves: "No one can take over my mind. Nothing can shake my faith and trust in God. No tragedy or loss can blind me to the goodness of God. I will be master here. I shall keep my thoughts calm and cheerful and always under my control."

Training the brain to concentrate is one of the best ways of teaching it to obey. Concentration means giving exclusive attention to a particular object and, as far as possible, allowing no other thought to enter the mind. The mere fact of realizing that your brain is an instrument you can use and command will help you to concentrate. Try to see yourself in possession of a power you can control and operate almost like an electric switch. You will become more accustomed to reason things out and to be less swayed by passing impulses and emotions. You will more easily reject harmful and unworthy thoughts.

We are what our thoughts are. The Bible tells us that a man *is* what he thinks in his heart. St. Paul gives us some relevant advice: "My brothers, your thoughts should be wholly directed to all that is true, all that deserves respect, all that is honest, pure, admirable, decent, virtuous, or worthy of praise" (Phil. 4:8).

The Stoics of ancient times excelled in the training and mastery of the mind to the extent that they were able to endure incredible hardships with calm fortitude. We are Christians. While we acknowledge the powerful capacities of the human brain, we realize its limitations, especially where God is concerned.

Several centuries ago, there lived a priest who was famed for his learning. He was St. Thomas Aquinas, and it is said of him that he used to dictate to three of his secretaries at once. His greatest work was called the "Summa"—a survey of all theology. One day during his Mass, he went into an ecstasy. It had happened before, but on this occasion the ecstasy lasted a long time. Afterwards, he said, "Such secrets have been revealed to me that all I have written now appears to be of little value." Great saints, like great artists, become aware of their inability to express the inner vision that has been granted them.

Without God's grace and His revealed knowledge to guide us, our brains may only make us clever devils. "Your attitude must be that of Christ...," says St. Paul (Phil. 2:5). If by regular and prayerful reflection on Christ's words we can make His thoughts our own, then we shall use our brain in the way our Maker intended us to use it—as a wonderful tool and instrument of our happiness now and hereafter.

The Enemy

Many people think that belief in the devil is a superstition of the past. They think that devil worship and diabolical possession are relics of the past, if indeed they ever existed.

But in December, 1971, a woman journalist stated that she was writing about the most frightening and deadly serious subject she had ever written about—the spread of satanic worship among the young. Since then, much has come to light on this subject, and the facts are horrifying.

The flourishing of teenage covens (gatherings of witches) is destroying many young people. In a world increasingly sickened and bored by material things, many of them are searching into the realms of black and white magic. Whereas a great many people today have only vague beliefs in God, or in the after-life, or in prayer, or in the devil, the worshipers of Satan are very different. They believe passionately and choose to follow the ways of Satan—perverted, cruel and wicked. The manifestations of an evil intelligence are all too common to be rejected as nonsense, and they often have recognizable features, such as intense cold and a pervading sense of evil.

It can happen so easily—an invitation to a party, some "innocent fun" with a Ouija board, some drug-taking, then an introduction to a room magnificent in its blackness, black walls, drapes and carpets, a robed priest at an altar with black candles, a crucifix turned upside down, an initiation rite, the peculiar chanting of the Lord's Prayer backwards, and then the sickeningly immoral and brutal acts....

Many youngsters, vulnerable and sensitive, are spiritually and emotionally destroyed, perverted, controlled and used by the immense telepathic power of the coven. It is thought that there are as many as 80,000 witches in Britain alone and thousands of young people accept completely that they must obey any orders given them by their satanic coven leaders. If they do not, they are convinced of being in deadly danger.

One man convicted of numerous sex attacks on children was a known dabbler in black magic. The judge who gave him a thirty-year jail sentence said of him, "He is a cunning and hideous man who appears to show no remorse or horror or emotion for the crimes he has perpetrated."

Baudelaire once said, "Satan's deepest wile is to persuade us he doesn't exist." Perhaps he is overplaying his hand at present. Certainly he is active in many subtle ways, but sometimes he comes into the open. Diabolical possession is a proof of the existence of the devils. Some modern critics say that people described in the Gospels as possessed by devils were in reality insane or subject to fits. But the writers of the Gospels often make a clear distinction between mental or physical illness and diabolical possession. The physician Luke says the crowds came to our Lord to "be healed of their diseases. Those who were troubled with unclean spirits were cured..." (Lk. 6:18). Christ expressly gives power to His disciples to cast out devils.

Diabolical possession still happens. Some years ago, a Jesuit teacher at the Catholic University in Calcutta told of being requested to exorcise a young Indian girl. She was completely illiterate, but when possessed spoke fluently in a foreign European language.

Exorcism is an ancient rite of the Church, and the climax of the ceremony comes when with upraised crucifix the priest blesses the person possessed and commands the evil spirit, "In the name of the Father, and of the Son and of the Holy Spirit, I charge you to come out and depart." The Jesuit said that when he came to these words, the girl screamed abuse and blasphemy and became so convulsed and contorted by a paroxysm of maniacal rage that he feared for the girl's life. It was only after more than a dozen attempts that he finally succeeded in freeing her.

What is diabolical possession? It is an imitation of the divine by Satan—a caricature of the Incarnation. As God took our human nature and lives in us and influences us by His indwelling and grace, the devil seeks to assert power over us, motivated not by love, but by a malevolent hatred which seeks our destruction.

Such possession is not animation, for the devil does not give life to the human body. But he gets control over the bodily senses. Thus he deprives the soul of its normal mastery and function; he seems to look out of the eyes of the possessed, distorting the face and speaking through the mouth.

There may be partial possession and there seem to be devils of different personality and power—devils of pride, of avarice, of anger, of hatred, of impurity and of deceit. Not all show the same malice and cruelty, nor do all have the same intelligence or power. Some are driven out with little trouble, never to return, but others resist and even when cast out, return again and again.

Over the years, case histories of diabolical possession have been gathered and some significant facts have emerged. The difficulty with which an evil spirit is sometimes exorcised might seem due to its reluctance to return to hell, but it may also be an unwillingness to leave until some act of destruction has been performed. In the Gospels, there is the instance when the devils beg to be allowed to pass into a herd of swine so as to destroy it.

The devils have a great dread of the crucifix, of the holy Name, and especially of our Lady. They are panic-stricken at any mention of Mary and recognize that her name prevails. This is a remarkably literal confirmation of the ancient prediction:

"I will put enmity between you and the woman,
and between your offspring and hers;
He will strike at your head..." (Gn. 3:15).

The powers of the devils are limited. If they were allowed to attack us when and to the extent they wished, we would no longer be free. They are powerful, but they are "chained dogs." None of us, however, is ever safely beyond their reach, so we always need to pray for God's help. Perhaps it was partly as a warning to us that Christ permitted Himself to be tempted. The saints were often tempted and troubled—not by possession, but by infestation.

St. John Vianney was sometimes attacked physically, and he said he always knew when a great sinner was coming to him for confession by the trouble the devil gave him. As she lay dying, St. Bernadette displayed a momentary fear. "Leave me, Satan," she was heard to say, and she recovered her equanimity. St. Teresa of Avila said, "I saw around me a great multitude of devils, and yet I seemed to be enveloped by a great light which prevented their coming near me...."

Such dreadful happenings as devil worship and diabolical possession are frightening reminders to us of the existence of a world of fallen and depraved spirits. They also remind us of our grave responsibility to use our God-given freedom well. For it is by the abuse of his freedom that a person can go to the terrible extremity of choosing to surrender his will to ultimate evil.

We have been warned. St. Paul centuries ago gave the alarm, "Put on the armor of God so that you may be able to stand firm against the tactics of the devil. Our battle is not against human forces but against the principalities and powers, the rulers of this world of darkness, the evil spirits in regions above" (Eph. 6:11-12).

St. Peter, the first Pope, never forgot our Lord's frightening admonition, "Get out of my sight, you satan!" (Mt. 16:23), nor his own cowardly denial of Christ: "Stay sober and alert. Your opponent the devil is prowling like a roaring lion looking for someone to devour. Resist him, solid in your faith..." (1 Pt. 5:8-9).

Pope Paul VI spoke of the devil as a "living spiritual being, which is perverted and perverting.... He is the number one enemy, the tempter without equal who sows errors and disasters in human history...."

Diabolical influences are all around us. We live in enemy-occupied territory. Many are deceived by the "father of lies" (Jn. 8:44), into thinking he no longer exists. Some no longer believe in the world of the spirits, in angels, good or bad, though the Bible and Christ Himself clearly speak of them.

"Deliver us from evil" is the final petition of the Lord's Prayer. We should say it more frequently and fervently. "When we have asked for God's protection against evil and have obtained it," says St. Cyprian, "then we stand secure and safe against everything which the devil and the world can do against us. For what fear is there in this life to the man whose guardian is God?"

The Torment of Temptation

He was an Englishman living just before Shakespeare's time and is recognized as one of the great Elizabethans. He took both degrees at Oxford University and was so brilliant that he received an appointment on the faculty at seventeen. He was handsome, gay and witty, and so elegant and eloquent that young men imitated his walk and mannerisms. He was called, "Oxford's diamond" and "England's Cicero," and Elizabeth herself told him to ask for whatever honor he wanted.

At first he was blinded by his success, but his keen mind later became troubled by scruples. After much anguish, he gave up his life of ease and went abroad to become a Jesuit. After ordination he returned to England, but such was his daring and zeal in reconciling lapsed Catholics and in making converts that he soon became a much-wanted fugitive. He was eventually betrayed, imprisoned and cruelly tortured. The queen personally intervened and offered to free him and to make him Archbishop of Canterbury if only he would renounce his Catholic Faith. He refused and was put to death. He is now known and venerated as St. Edmund Campion.

All temptation is a kind of suffering and torture. It is an ordeal and a torment amounting almost to martyrdom. It is an attempt to force the human will, a solicitation to an evil that is known and recognized as evil but which is also powerfully attractive.

Temptations are our inevitable lot. "The spirit is willing, but nature is weak," Christ said (Mt. 26:41).

"The flesh lusts against the spirit," wrote St. Paul (Gal. 5:17). "I cannot even understand my own actions. I do not do what I want to do but what I hate" (Rom. 7:15).

Animals follow the instincts of their animal nature. Chesterton said, "You can slap a man on the back and tell him to be a man, but there is no use slapping a crocodile on its back and telling it to be a crocodile." Animals live, as it were, on lower ground, but human beings are meant to scale the heights.

Not only is temptation not a sin, but it can be argued that if temptation were removed, then life as we know it would be the poorer without it. Temptation is a test and a challenge. In Greek, the same word is used for "trial" and "temptation." Christ permitted Himself to be tempted by Satan in the wilderness while He was fasting and praying, and again in the Garden of Gethsemani and on Calvary. Temptations are, therefore, not evil in themselves but are a part of our training and development.

Christ allowed Himself to be tempted to show us He is truly human and that temptation in itself is not sin. "For we do not have a high priest who is unable to sympathize with our weakness, but one who was tempted in every way that we are, yet never sinned" (Heb. 4:15).

Doubtless Christ also permitted those mysterious temptations of Himself as an example to us of how we are to deal with them. "Away with you, Satan!" (Mt. 4:10) Our Lord shows us the absolute necessity of prompt rejection of temptation. In this respect, how true is the old adage, "He who hesitates is lost."

Pierre D'Harcourt was a young member of the French Resistance Movement who was betrayed and spent two years in solitary confinement in Fresnes prison. At the very outset, he knew he would have to be strict with himself if he were to keep his sanity. "There were not many things I could do. I would avoid some habits, thinking about women and that kind of thing. Thinking even of my home was disastrous. I felt very often that if I went on thinking along those lines, it would be absolutely impossible. I would collapse."

Many of the American prisoners of war returning after long years of imprisonment in North Vietnam described the strict mental discipline they imposed on themselves which, together with prayer and solidarity with one another, enabled them to resist the temptation to surrender to their captors' unjust demands.

Where evil is concerned, we are all in a "Resistance Movement" and our rejection of temptation will have greater chance of success if we turn away from it as soon as we recognize it. We must learn to act promptly against all thoughts of hatred, pride, impurity and discouragement before they can take hold of our mind and imagination.

We must be equally vigilant with regard to occasions of sin and our limitations and propensities. In the Tower of London, there is a flight of stone steps leading to one of the high turrets. All the steps are exactly the same size until the top one is reached; this one is a few inches higher than the others. Used here is a simple strategy based on the assumption that people have the habit of taking things for granted. An unsuspecting assailant would climb the steps successfully, but be unprepared for that last higher one. He would stumble and be at the mercy of the waiting defender. "Let anyone who thinks he is standing upright watch out lest he fall!" (1 Cor. 10:12)

We need to watch our step. Appearances are often tempting and deceptive. As Shakespeare puts it, "Bait the hook well, this fish will bite." Temptations are meant to be alluring. Our Lord was constantly warning His disciples to be watchful and prepared. "Be on guard, and pray that you may not undergo the test" (Mt. 26:41).

Temptations make prayer necessary. If the body is deprived of food, its resistance to disease is weakened. Prayer is spiritual nourishment, but the nourishment needs to be taken regularly. Regular prayer is essential. In times of trial, we shall turn more easily to prayer if we have the habit of regular prayer.

Temptations may trouble and torment us, but we can be sure God will not allow us to be tempted beyond our powers of endurance and He will help us, providing we do what is required of us. "No man," said William James, "has matriculated in the university of life until he has been well tempted." It is because we are free to do right or wrong that we are tempted and are therefore worthy of praise or blame. We should never be discouraged when we are tempted or even when we sometimes yield to temptation. God will not despise a humble and contrite heart.

A Stradivarius violin is worth many thousands of dollars. Its tone is purer and sweeter than when it left the workshop two hundred and fifty years ago. It is said that when the Italian craftsman chose wood from which to fashion his violins, he always selected that part of the tree that had faced the north. Stradivarius declared that the part that had withstood wind and weather invariably produced the loveliest music. How often do we find that the kindest, bravest and gentlest people are those on whom the north winds of a hard life have blown, those whose faith and goodness have been tried and tested!

Temptation is not so much the affliction and penalty of men and women as it is their privilege and glory. St. James even says that there is a special beatitude for the tempted: "Happy the man who holds out to the end through trial! Once he has been proved, he will receive the crown of life" (Jas. 1:12).

Do We Doubt?

Doubts can be disturbing and harmful. They weaken and destroy our relationships with others—as when we doubt someone's sincerity or honesty or love. Doubts can paralyze our activity. Shakespeare said, "Our doubts are traitors and make us lose the good we oft might win, by fearing to attempt."

To have religious doubts, to doubt the existence of God and the after-life, is surely an unhappy state. The agnostic who claims we can know nothing outside the material world builds his life upon doubt, but to be fully happy, life must be positive and purposive. "Give me your faith!" cried Goethe. "I have doubts enough of my own."

Yet doubts we all have and they are unavoidable. If you wanted to avoid all doubt you would have to stop thinking, feeling, believing and striving, and this would be to stop living. In life as we know it, nothing is all black or all white, all bad or all good. Doubts, therefore, are a condition of growth and development; they are like growing pains. Dostoevsky said, "My hosanna has passed through the great purgatory of doubt." The important thing is not to remain in doubt, but to pass through it. Doubt is no more meant to be a permanent state than purgatory or growing pains.

The Bible has many instances of good people doubting. Moses doubted and was forbidden entrance to the Promised Land. Zechariah, the father of John the Baptist, doubted and was struck dumb.

When Christ taught the doctrine of the Eucharist, that He was the living bread come down from heaven and would give His flesh as food, some of His followers asked, "How can this be?" They persisted in their doubt and left Him.

The classic example of doubting is St. Thomas the apostle, 'doubting Thomas.' Recently he was referred to as the saint for the twentieth century, either because this is a century of colossal religious doubt, or because Thomas seems to typify modern men and women. He appears to have been a very matter-of-fact and down-to-earth kind of man. Near the end of the public ministry, when hostility was mounting against Him, Christ spoke of going to Bethany, close to Jerusalem. This was the danger zone, as the disciples knew. "'Rabbi,' protested the disciples, 'with the Jews only recently trying to stone you, you are going back up there again?'" (Jn. 11:8) But Thomas said: "Let us go along, to die with him" (Jn. 11:16).

When our Lord spoke of His Father's house of many mansions, He added:

> "I am indeed going to prepare a place for you, and then I shall come back to take you with me, that where I am you also may be.
> You know the way that leads where I go" (Jn. 14:3-4).

Thomas, down-to-earth as ever, was not satisfied: "'Lord,' said Thomas, 'we do not know where you are going. How can we know the way?'" (Jn. 14:5)

"I am the way, and the truth, and the life," Christ replied (Jn. 14:6).

And so while the others were convinced of Christ's resurrection, Thomas wanted to be sure himself. "I will never believe it without probing the nailprints in his hands, without putting my finger in the nailmarks and my hand into his side" (Jn. 20:25).

There is much for us to learn in Christ's reply to Thomas, after He showed the doubting apostle the place of His wounds:

> "Blest are they who have not seen and have believed" (Jn. 20:29).

Clearly God wants from us above all the surrender and submission of our faith and trust. Nor is it an unreasonable demand. Just because you can't explain a thing is no reason to doubt or deny it. Our hosannas will rise all the stronger and more triumphantly when they have passed through the purgatory of doubt. Our love will have been purified and perfected.

Then there is comfort for us in this incident of Thomas' doubt from the fact that Christ seeks him out, scarcely blaming him, and understanding the anguish Thomas suffers. It is one more instance of Christ showing concern for the individual. We all want to be known and loved as individual persons, but when we think of the millions of the human race, we could be tempted to doubt that God cares for each one of us.

But there is also a *warning* for us in Thomas' doubting. We do not know why he was not with the other apostles when Christ had appeared to them after

His resurrection. Thomas had left the group for some reason. Those who cut themselves off from the Church do so only to be lost in a wilderness of doubt. Goethe was right: "Give me your faith." We are strengthened by others' faith and we in turn can strengthen their faith.

Finally, this little event gives us assurance. All the doubts of Thomas disappear in the presence of the living Christ, the Son of God. We too, by our persevering prayer, the Mass and the sacraments, can have first-hand experience of the presence and power of the living Christ.

May we, then, never be disturbed or discouraged by doubts. No one can or even needs to be sure of everything. The captain of a ship bringing his vessel into port through a mist or darkness does not need to see all the streets and buildings along the shore. If he can make out one or two prominent landmarks, he can proceed with confidence. We have the great landmarks and certainties of our Catholic Faith—the mercy and goodness of God our Father; Christ our Lord and His Church; the Holy Spirit; God's grace, the sacraments, and prayer; our Lady and the saints; Christian doctrine and moral teachings.

Sometimes St. Paul experienced doubt about less important things, but he was always unwavering in his conviction about what really mattered: "We know that God makes all things work together for the good of those who have been called according to his decree" (Rom. 8:28). "I know him in whom I have believed..." (2 Tm. 1:12). "For I am certain that neither death nor life, neither angels nor principalities, neither the present nor the future, nor powers, neither height nor depth nor any other creature, will be able to separate us from the love of God that comes to us in Christ Jesus, our Lord" (Rom. 8:38-39). Sometimes in this doubting, disbelieving age of ours, we may have to pray humbly as the man in the Gospel prayed, "I do believe! Help my lack of trust!" (Mk. 9:24). But always at Mass, we should resolutely set our doubts aside and say wholeheartedly, "My Lord and my God" (Jn. 20:28). It is then that we are in the presence of the living Christ, who is for us, as He was for Thomas, "the way, the truth and the life" (Jn. 14:6).

A Personal Faith

There is an interesting little story about one of the statues at Lourdes. The statue portrays a blind man who has just recovered his sight. The cure of the blind man was one of the first miracles at Lourdes, but the statue is in remembrance of an altogether different event.

It was erected many years ago by a lady who chanced to be passing through Lourdes on her way to a fashionable seaside resort. Out of curiosity, she stayed in the little town. She was a Catholic, but some years previously when her husband had died, she had lost all belief in God. At Lourdes she regained her faith and the statue was a thank-offering. On it is the inscription: "To recover faith is a greater miracle than to recover sight."

Sometimes people think that faith consists merely in believing a lot of dry doctrines and mechanically reciting creeds. If this were all that being a Christian meant, the Christian Faith would be valueless because it would be abstract and coldly intellectual. Faith is deeply personal and mysterious. It is belief on the authority of another. The Christian Faith is not primarily a relationship to statements and things, but to a Person.

It is Christ Himself, the founder of Christianity, who has made it so and who always emphasizes this personal element.

"I came
that they might have life..." (Jn. 10:10).
"All this I tell you
that my joy may be yours
and your joy may be complete" (Jn. 15:11).
"Come to me, all you who are weary and find life burdensome, and I will refresh you" (Mt. 11:28). "I am the good shepherd..." (Jn. 10:11). "I am the bread that came down from heaven..."(Jn. 6:41). "I am the resurrection and the life..."(Jn. 11:25). Do you believe I can do this...do you believe in me? (cf. Jn. 11:26).

Faith, then, is not just the acceptance of a doctrine, but of the reality expressed in the doctrine. The Christian Faith is the total acceptance of Christ and through Him, belief in the Trinity, the Church and all other revealed teachings.

The Christian Faith is not just emotion. We say, "I believe" and not "I feel," because our faith is knowledge. It has this in common with most of our ordinary knowledge: it is not self-evident, for we have it on the authority of others.

One of the greatest joys of life is the happiness and satisfaction we get from knowledge and from sharing it with other people. The mind is made to know; it thirsts for knowledge; it cannot rest; it is always active. You cannot think of "nothing." Deprived of knowledge, the mind can become deranged, as sometimes happens with people kept for a long time in solitary confinement.

The Christian Faith brings knowledge that is a joy and support in life. How often people who have been crushed under some overwhelming suffering have declared, "It was only my Faith that saved me."

A woman patient said to Professor Jung, the psychiatrist: "If only I knew that my life had some purpose or meaning! Then there would be no silly story about my nerves."

It is precisely because faith is knowledge that creeds and doctrines are necessary. They are statements that enshrine the divine truths and guard them from error. Doctrines are necessary in much the same way as the bone structure is essential for the body. A skeleton is not a particularly attractive object, but without our bone structure, we could not exist.

It is obvious too, that faith needs nourishing if it is to be kept alive. Religious beliefs do not automatically stay in the mind. It is safe to say that almost all who have lost their belief in Christianity have not been reasoned out of it by honest argument, but have simply drifted away from the Faith. Like the seed in Christ's parable, the faith has withered through neglect or been choked out of existence.

We can only cherish what we know. Even greater knowledge of a daisy will increase our appreciation of this lowly plant.

Some people get very sentimental about religion, even in this scientific age. They want religion to be completely simple, to be just "love" and "joy." Christianity *is* joyous love, but it is something more. Cardinal Newman said, "We must not preach just love, but holiness." C. S. Lewis wrote:

"People who want a simple religion are being unrealistic. Nothing that is real is simple—looking at a table may seem very simple, but a scientist would have much to tell you of what is entailed, of how the object is composed of atoms, of how light waves rebound from it and what they do to the optic nerve and of how impressions are conveyed to the brain...." We must then never forget that theology is a science and that faith is fundamentally knowledge, and not just moods and emotions.

How do we clothe the bone structure of creed and doctrine so that our faith becomes a living, personal relationship with God? First, we must pray to have stronger faith. The human mind, for all its great achievements, cannot rise to the supernatural unless it is aided by God. Flesh and blood are not enough. We must humbly acknowledge our need. "I do believe! Help my lack of trust!" (Mk. 9:24)

Next we must exercise our faith. We must live it. "Faith without works is as dead as a body without breath" (Jas. 2:26). We live our faith when we perform good deeds of kindness, when we resist temptation, when we are patient in suffering and when we persevere unaffected by the unbelief and worldliness around us.

Finally, we must endeavor to have a living, personal faith in Christ. If you really believe in something, it becomes a part of you and you care desperately about it. This was how it was with St. Paul, "The life I live now is not my own; Christ is living in me" (Gal. 2:20). The Christian's credo means in effect, "I believe in You, Lord Jesus; I believe in all Your words and promises. I really care about You and I trust and love You. You have the words of eternal life. May I never be parted from You."

Mainstay of Life

A large European Catholic magazine published a pathetic letter describing a family struck by polio and cancer, poverty and utter despair. The readers responded with overwhelming generosity to the father's plea. Moreover, to their material help, many added words of Christian comfort and encouragement.

"Now I know God has not forgotten us!" the grateful man wrote. "We don't feel alone anymore. For the first time in many months, we can hope again."

In times of trial and anxious suspense, we sometimes encourage one another with the words Cicero spoke centuries ago, "While there is life, there is hope." But perhaps it is more correct to say, "While there is hope there is life." When hope is gone, life is finished. "Hope is the only tie that keeps the heart from breaking." Every normal and average life has its quota of monotonous routine, difficulties and disappointments, and hope is the driving force that enables us to plod along. "The miserable," says Shakespeare, "have no other medicine but hope."

Although it is concerned with the future, hope is founded on remembrance. We recall past goodness and happiness, and hope results. Dante said, "There is no greater grief than in misery to recall happier times." This is true, but the memory of happier times can comfort us and help us to believe that happy times can come again. "Your old men shall dream dreams," said Joel, the prophet (Jl. 3:1). If our dreams of the past leave us sad and regretful, it is not a good thing. But if we gratefully recall the happiness and blessings of former days, we are more likely to have a well-founded hope for the future.

In the Old Testament, Jacob is the great hero of hope, just as Abraham is of faith. Jacob was a "simple man, who kept to his tents"(Gn. 25:27). He had a gentle, affectionate nature. He was something of a dreamer, easily upset and frightened, but always reassured by the remembrance of God's mercies to him in the past. Patiently he waited and served seven years to marry Rachel—"yet they seemed to him but a few days because of his love for her"(Gn. 29:20). Waiting is usually tedious and wearisome and only hope can make it endurable.

Jacob's life was hard, but he gratefully remembered God's goodness. "I am unworthy of all the acts of kindness that you have loyally performed..." (Gn. 32:11). This is the pattern: remembrance of God's goodness, mercies, and the promises He made in the past.

Hope is the theme of the New Testament, of the "good news," the Gospel. Christ revived the hopes of mankind. He is our hope.

After His resurrection, Jesus encountered the two dejected disciples on the road to Emmaus and listened to them. "We were hoping that he was the one who would set Israel free" (Lk. 24:21). Our Lord rebuked them—they had forgotten. "What little sense you have! How slow you are to believe all that the prophets have announced! Did not the Messiah have to undergo all this so as to enter into his glory?"(Lk. 24:25-26). He succeeded in reviving their hope by recalling the past: "Beginning, then, with Moses and all the prophets, he interpreted for them every passage of Scripture which referred to him" (Lk. 24:27).

"In hope we were saved" (Rom. 8:24), says St. Paul. We need to cherish and cultivate the virtue of hope; it is one of God's most precious gifts. A facile, cheery optimism is not enough. There are times in life when everything seems hopeless and futile. There are times when such a dark cloud of misery surrounds us that all goodness and beauty are obliterated and it seems useless and impossible to go on living. Nor is it enough to have our hopes focused on any earthly horizon alone—what Shakespeare calls "a high hope for a low heaven." "If our hopes in Christ are limited to this life only," says St. Paul, "we are the most pitiable of men"(1 Cor. 15:19). We need a Christian hope—hope given us by God and based on God's goodness and power, revealed to us in Christ. St. Paul sums it up for us when he tells us to remember Jesus Christ.

In a play by a French playwright is a scene where Pilate, old and retired, is reminiscing with a friend. Suddenly the friend asks, "Do you remember that young man who was crucified in Jerusalem?" Pilate ponders thoughtfully and then shakes his head. "Tell me more about him."

"He was a religious leader...his followers were mostly poor people. He himself was from Nazareth... yes, that was his name, Jesus of Nazareth." Pilate rubs his chin reflectively, probing his memory, and then says, "No, I cannot remember him," and the talk passes on to other subjects.

Pilate had forgotten Christ. This may seem fanciful and far-fetched. But is it? When we become skeptical and cynical, when we are depressed, lose heart and give way to despair, is it not simply because we have forgotten Jesus Christ? It is for our sakes that our Lord wants us to remember Him. "Do this as a remembrance of me"(Lk. 22:19).

"If I forget you, Jerusalem,
may my right hand be forgotten!"(Ps. 137:5)

We ought often to recall God's mercies and favors, lest they become "benefits forgot." Like Jacob, we should love to dwell on happy memories, remembering the times and the seasons, giving thanks for this and that grace and blessing—good parents, a happy home, health, friends, and the countless small enjoyments in our lives. Recall all the good that was given us, and yes, even what was taken away for some reason we may never know. This we do know, however: God is good and He never ceases to cherish us, His dear children, who are not worthy of the least of His acts of kindness.

Above all, we will remember Jesus Christ, His goodness, power and mercy, and all His assurances and promises. "Hope is the mainstay of my life," said Pope St. Pius X. "Hope is my unfailing strength in doubt, the strong support of my weakness; hope, but not in man; hope in Christ who is able to uphold the weakest. God refuses no grace to those who trust in Him. O hope, hope, which unites me to God, and God to me!"

Transforming Love

The word "love" is constantly in use and although it describes something that is noble and inestimable, it is often grossly misused. The husband who leaves his wife and children to go off with another woman says he does it out of love. The peddler of narcotics and the revolutionary who plants bombs that kill innocent people call themselves "freedom lovers." The burglar who steals diamonds for his girl-friend, the woman who urges her husband to gain power and prestige unlawfully, and even the mother who over-indulges her children, making them unfit for life—all say they are motivated by love.

Love needs intelligent guidance and wise control; otherwise it will degenerate and become destructive. Like fear, love can get out of hand. To say that the heart has its reasons is nonsense, because the heart does not reason.

Of all the arts, music might seem to be the most emotional, yet it is said that the best music comes from the brain. Great composers work like mathematicians.

We are commanded,

"'You shall love the Lord your God...
with all your mind'" (Mt. 22:37).

In His wonderful talk on love at the Last Supper, Christ says three times,

"He who obeys the commandments he has
from me
is the man who loves me..." (Jn. 14:21).

For all its abuse, love is the greatest power and driving force in existence. It is an amazing, transforming power.

Even the "love" shown by a devoted pet is touching. One January morning some years ago, an eighty-year-old shepherd living in the north of England left his home to walk in the hills he knew and loved so well. He never returned, and when his body was found six weeks later, his dog was still with him, emaciated, but alive. It had endured great hunger and cold. In its own way the animal was still faithful and devoted.

Even more remarkable is the story of "Elsa," the African lioness, tamed by Mr. and Mrs. Adamson. A strange feature of this instance of a notoriously ferocious animal being tamed by love is that after the lioness was fully grown, had returned to the wild life of the jungle and had mated, its affection for the brave and understanding Adamsons still remained, for it allowed them to approach its young. Their kind treatment had had a lasting effect.

Divine love, or grace, as it is called, has an infinitely more transforming effect upon our human nature. God is love; it is His very nature, and His love of us raises us so that we share His nature. St. John says,

"We, for our part, love
because he first loved us" (1 Jn. 4:19).

We are sharers of the divine nature much as the drops of water are absorbed into the wine of the chalice in the Mass. A rebirth is effected by the sacrament of Baptism. The water of the sacrament symbolizes life—a waterless land is a desert. The word "life" abounds in the Gospels and this sharing in the divine nature is the fullness of life, of grace and of love which Christ claimed to have brought us.

It is important for us to understand this so as to realize the grandeur of divine love: "If only you recognized God's gift" (Jn. 4:10). Human love can have a spiritually transforming effect upon us; people in love do change. But divine love makes a more radical change. It elevates our nature.

It is essential to be reborn, but this is not enough. There must be a continuous dying to self; there must be prayer and self-denial. The gardener has to prune and remove the useless wood so as to promote growth, let in light and air and increase the fruit yield. God is the gardener of our souls. Almost the first thing He told Abraham was to leave all and come away. And Christ said, "Whoever wishes to be my follower must deny his very self, take up his cross each day, and follow in my steps" (Lk. 9:23).

All this is in conflict with the sloppy, sentimental talk about love emanating even from some pulpits today. It is only by a rather painful process that an animal becomes domesticated. By nature most are wild, predatory and dirty. If we wish to train them to live with us, we must correct them, discipline them, and teach them to be clean. All this is contrary to their nature, but eventually they are fit to share our homes and the happiness of human companionship.

It is much the same in our relationship with God. The transformation He requires of us is painful—all change is painful—but it is essential that we should lose our selfishness and pride, our worldliness and pettiness. There can be no transfigurement without some disfigurement. But transformation *is* possible. The hairy, unsightly caterpillar weaving a cocoon around itself and emerging a fragile butterfly illustrates this change. God's love and grace enveloping us can completely transform us.

This divine, transforming love should be everything to us. "If only you recognized God's gift..." (Jn. 4:10). If we did indeed know God's new creation, His most precious gift, sanctifying grace, then we would turn more resolutely from temptation and sin. We would submit more patiently and trustingly to God's will. We would be more concerned with prayer and more attentive to the needs of others. We must seek to preserve this gift, this love which transforms our weak nature and makes us patient and kind: "There is no limit to love's forbearance, to its trust, its hope, its power to endure" (1 Cor. 13:7).

We Must See Jesus

A few days before Christ died, a little incident occurred in Jerusalem. So many big events were taking place at the time and the incident was so small that it is remarkable St. John remembered it and afterwards wrote about it in his Gospel.

It was a period of mounting tension. Our Lord's popularity was at its peak as a result of His raising Lazarus to life. But the hostility of His enemies was also increasing: "If we let him go on like this, the whole world will believe in him" (Jn. 11:48). The hour of final confrontation was drawing near.

Just at this time, some Greek-speaking strangers arrived in the city. They approached Philip, one of the apostles, with a courteous request: "Sir, we should like to see Jesus," they said (Jn. 12:21). If ever a universal need was put briefly and simply, it was surely in these words. "Seeing is believing," we say, and this is true because sight gives us reassurance; without it, we grope in uncertainty and lack full knowledge.

Expressions such as "I am longing to see you"; "I must see the doctor"; "I want to see for myself" are constantly in use, and they are echoed in the Gospels with reference to Christ. "Let us go over to Bethlehem and see this event which the Lord has made known to us" (Lk. 2:15). "Where is the newborn king of the Jews? We observed his star at its rising and have come to pay him homage" (Mt. 2:2).

"We have seen his glory:
The glory of an only Son coming from the Father..." (Jn. 1:14).
"Now, Master, you can dismiss your servant in peace....
For my eyes have witnessed your saving deed..." (Lk. 2:29-30).

Christ Himself said, "Blest are the eyes that see what you see" (Lk. 10:23).

In the days of Christ there were many who were blinded by pride and self-interest and failed utterly to see and recognize Him. But countless men and women did see Him and their lives were changed by what they saw. Nicodemus, wealthy and educated; Magdalene, possessed, it was said, by seven devils; Zacchaeus, the little tax-gatherer, climbing a tree for a better view; a thief dying on a cross—all kinds of people were profoundly affected by the sight of Jesus. The very fact that the Gospels were not written until many years after Christ's death and yet so much about Him is vividly recorded shows how profound and lasting was the impression made by our Lord upon those who saw Him.

Someone has said that you can read Shakespeare or the words of any great writer and you may be entertained and enlightened, but read the Gospels and you will be filled with awe and respect. You will be challenged, profoundly influenced and changed.

We must see Jesus. This does not mean seeing Him with our bodily eyes. Even the many beautiful paintings of Christ somehow leave us unmoved, perhaps because we are seeing Him through another's eyes, not our own. To see Jesus means to see Him with the eyes of the mind, to know Him. This is not easy.

How difficult it is even to know the people around us! Each of us is different. How can we analyze the tangled web of thoughts, emotions, and stored-up experiences that lie beneath the compact covering of flesh and blood? How difficult even to know ourselves!

"If we could only see ourselves as others see us,
it would from many an error free us."

How much more difficult to see Christ, to know that supremely mysterious Person who is both God and man! The strangest and most conflicting errors have been made about Him.

Many people fail to see Him as being truly God. They are blind to those stupendous claims He clearly made: the claim to have equality of nature with His Father; the claim to be the fulfillment of the ancient messianic prophecies; the claim to be the Savior of mankind, the pardoner of sin, the giver of eternal life; the claim to have all power in heaven and on earth—claims that no other living being has ever made and substantiated.

Many have erred about His character and personality. To the founders of certain groups, He appeared grimly stern and frightening, hard and unyielding. But this is not how the Gospels portray Him, nor how ordinary men and women saw Him. "The majority of the crowd heard this [His words] with delight" (Mk. 12:37). "At the sight of the Lord the disciples rejoiced" (Jn. 20:20). Would little children have thronged confidently about Him if He had been unsmiling and severe? Even the slanderous accusation that He was "a glutton and drunkard, a lover of tax collectors and those outside the law!" (Mt. 11:19), is a proof of our Lord's approachability and His friendliness to all kinds of people.

On the other hand, there are those who see Christ as weak and sentimental, the meek and gentle shepherd, the idealist unacquainted with the harsh realities of life. It is true that He was humble and compassionate, but He was never permissive or afraid or weakly indulgent. No one spoke such encouraging, forgiving words to repentant sinners as did Christ, but no one ever said such terrible things about sin and its consequences as He did.

Always His words are an unequivocal challenge:

"Anyone who loves me
will be true to my word" (Jn. 14:23).

"None of those who cry out, 'Lord, Lord,' will enter the kingdom of God but only the one who does the will of my Father in heaven" (Mt. 7:21). "He who will not take up his cross and come after me is not worthy of me" (Mt. 10:38). Had Christ been a weak, sentimental and ineffective character, He would have been forgotten long ago and He would never have influenced the lives of countless millions as He has.

We must see Jesus. It is vitally important, for if we would know God, we must see Jesus first.

"Whoever has seen me has seen the Father" (Jn. 14:9).

If we want to know the meaning of life, we must see Him who has declared,

"I am the way, and the truth, and the life..." (Jn. 14:6).

If we want to be shown how to lead a holy and happy life, how to practice the difficult virtues of submission and trust, patience and self-sacrificing love, we must see Him who has said, "...learn from me..." (Mt. 11:29).

How can we see Jesus best? We must live with Him. You can read or hear about a place, but you do not really know it until you have lived in it. You can know about people, but you only really know them when you have lived with them. Christ's last words to His apostles are full of exhortations to abide in Him. And to give us the means to do this, He instituted the Eucharist.

We live with Christ when we reflect often upon His words and deeds, upon His teaching and upon His example as given us in the Gospels; when we read what holy and learned people have written about Him, and especially when we are guided by His Church. We live with Him when we strive to live like Him in the avoidance of sin and all self-seeking. Even slight sins cloud our vision of Christ.

"Blest are the single-hearted
for they shall see God" (Mt. 5:8).

We live with Him when we live in Him—in the hidden mysterious life of grace, in our prayer-life and in our Holy Communions.

"What do you want...?" Christ asked the man who had been born blind. "Rabboni,...I want to see" (Mk. 10:51). How privileged he was, for when his dead eyes came alive, he looked into the very face of the Son of God. This must be our desire and prayer, or else we shall grope uncertainly through life. We must seek to see Jesus in the commonplace things of everyday life, in our sorrows as in our joys, in our tasks and duties, and in our neighbor, so that one day we shall achieve our destiny, which is to "...see him as he is" (1 Jn. 3:2).

Who Do You Say I Am?

There is an old story about the famous tightrope walker, Blondin, whose daring feats of balance thrilled the world. One of his most spectacular acts was to walk across a rope stretched above Niagara Falls, where a mistake meant certain death. On one occasion he turned to a boy who stood by, breathless with admiration: "Do you believe I could carry someone across on my shoulders?" Above the roar of the Falls, the boy's shouted reply sounded exultant: "Yes, I *know* you could, sir!" But when Blondin offered to take him, the boy shrank back, afraid.

The story illustrates Christ's attitude and approach to the people of His day. It was a personal approach. "Who do you say that I am?" (Mt. 16:15) "Are you confident I can do this?" (Mt. 9:28) "Do you want to leave me too?" (Jn. 6:67) The very term "follower" implies a freedom of choice.

First there must be knowledge of Him before there can be acceptance. We must know a person before we can love him.

Christ challenges us as no one else has done in history. Every sane-minded person acknowledges that He did exist and that His teaching is not mere sloppy idealism. But there are millions of people who are uncertain about Him and wonder whether He is really God or just a wise and holy man.

There can be no doubt but that He Himself made the astonishing and unequivocable claim to be God:

"'I am God's Son'" (Jn. 10:36);

"Before Abraham came to be, I AM" (Jn. 8:58). The Hebrew words "I am" were the name of God, and according to Jewish law, to utter them was blasphemy deserving of death. Equally clear is Jesus' reply to the High Priest's questioning at His trial: "Are you the Messiah, the Son of the Blessed One?" "I am; and you will see the Son of Man seated at the right hand of the Power and coming with the clouds of heaven" (Mk. 14:61, 62).

Apart from these plain statements, it must be admitted that Christ's identity was shrouded in mystery. He was something of a mystery even to His closest followers. Impatiently, they once demanded of Him, "If you really are the Messiah, tell us so in plain words" (Jn. 10:24). They knew, of course, that He was quite unique in their experience, that He was altogether different from any other religious leader or prophet.

They must have noticed, for instance, that while He exhorted them to pray, He never asked them to pray *for* Him, but on the contrary, He encouraged them to pray *to* Him. They observed, too, how He always spoke with authority. The Old Testament teachers had never spoken in their own name; it was always, "So says the Lord."

In the Gospels Jesus speaks and acts as though authority belongs to Him personally: "I forgive you," "I say to you." He casts out devils in His own name and performs miracles by His own power. He is more than familiar with the world about Him because He knows the fears, the hopes and the questionings hidden in human hearts. But He is equally familiar with the supernatural world. He speaks of the angels in heaven rejoicing over repentant sinners, of His Father and divine Providence, of heaven itself. And always He speaks naturally, on His own authority, as if He were merely stating the obvious and the factual. The statements seem to slip out almost inadvertently.

But the mystery remains and it is largely a mystery of His own making. At His transfiguration He says, "Do not tell anyone of the vision" (Mt. 17:9). When the devils cry out that He is the Son of God, He sternly silences them. He often enjoins secrecy on those He has cured of disease.

Does He weaken His case by this mystery? No. In fact, He shows He is not an impostor, for He doesn't, like an impostor, "protest overmuch." Nor is He "touchy" and aggressive in His claims. Furthermore, He shows He is not a madman suffering from hallucinations, for such a one constantly dwells on his obsessions and acts insanely because of them. On the contrary, Christ's references to His Godhead are almost incidental; they are infrequent and indirect. He acts with restraint, with calm and wisdom.

Why then this secrecy with His followers? His ways are not always ours, but often they are very similar. A personal relationship must be free. Friendship and love cannot be forced. And so He did not blind His disciples with the truth about Himself. He gradually revealed Himself, slowly developing the relationship between them and Him, schooling and disposing them to receive the gift of faith, even leaving them some room for uncertainty so that they might learn to trust Him and take Him at His word.

Flesh and blood, mere worldly wisdom, wishes and feelings are not enough: "I offer you praise, O Father, Lord of heaven and earth, because what you have hidden from the learned and the clever you have revealed to the merest children" (Lk. 10:21).

His approach to each of us is no different. He makes a personal appeal and challenge. "...who do you say that I am?" (Mt. 16:15) He will not force the frail barrier of our free will. There will always be mystery surrounding Christ, for He is God.

We must be humble and patient because to know Christ will take time, effort and perhaps even suffering. But we should be deeply thankful that He makes such an appeal to us because it shows He loves us and desires our love, trust, and complete abandonment in Him.

The Meaning of the Hidden Life

Perhaps sometimes we have daydreamed about what we would do if we had our life to live all over again. Doubtless we would choose and arrange many things differently, but basically, our lives would probably be much the same—if only for the reason that our freedom of choice is restricted. We do not choose our parentage and birthplace, our temperament, natural gifts or defects, or our upbringing.

With Christ it was different. These are the very things He deliberately chose: His Mother, His birthplace, the circumstances of His upbringing, and every detail of His life and its surroundings. If He were to live His life over again, He would not choose to have anything different. He would live the same life of poverty, hardship and toil.

Obviously, we cannot know the whole reason for such a choice. All life is a mystery—our own and that of the world we live in. Much less do we understand the mysterious life of the Son of God. St. Paul says, "Now we see indistinctly, as in a mirror," and "My knowledge is imperfect now" (1 Cor. 13:12).

Writers have often pondered over those thirty hidden years of Christ's life. Many who disbelieve His divinity see them as a proof that our Lord was no more than a good man who only gradually realized that He had an important mission as a teacher of life. But we know that Christ's hidden life on earth had a special meaning and importance. He came for our sake, He lived His life for our salvation; therefore, those hidden years must have some bearing upon the lives of each one of us. We do not need to romanticize the life at Nazareth, but merely to try to see it as it was in reality.

Palestine in the time of Christ was a small country, about 150 by 75 miles, and was divided into three provinces: Judea, Samaria and Galilee. In an agreeable climate, fruit grew everywhere and was plentiful; the wealthy Roman ladies were always ready to pay a little extra for Palestinian grapes, olives, dates and figs.

But everything depended on hard work in which women and children took their share. When the harvest was bad, everyone suffered. Ordinarily, the poorer people had just two meals a day, and for a family to eat meat was a rare experience. The wage of a working man was only a few cents a day, and actual hunger would often invade the home, a hunger which threatened life.

Some houses were built of stone, but the poor lived in cave-like homes that had been hollowed out of the limestone hills. These consisted of two rooms in which a goat and chickens lived with the family. The water was drawn from the communal well around which village life was centered, but the animated discussions there would be no more than petty village gossip. "A village is a hive of glass, where nothing unobserved can pass."

A small country, an obscure mountain village, a tiny primitive home and a drab, dull life of hardship and drudgery—did the Son of God, the Savior of mankind, feel restricted and frustrated, repelled and wearied by it all? Nowadays, frequently asked questions about almost anything are "What's it good for? Is it relevant?" How could Christ's hidden life be relevant to the salvation of mankind? Why did He not come as the Jews of His time expected the Messiah to come, as a fully-grown, powerful and influential leader?

There are two important factors of our human existence that offer some explanation and understanding of Christ's choice. They are home and altar. Men have died to defend and preserve them. They are closely linked, and they fulfill our deepest human needs—security and love, peace and happiness.

Home stands for the cheering warmth and peace of a happily united family. The altar symbolizes the self-sacrificing love that both binds a family together and gives it the security of God's blessings and protection.

Those thirty years at Nazareth were not wasted, nor were they meaningless. Christ lived them in order to teach mankind the importance of home and family life. It is the family, not just the walls and roof, that makes a true home: father, mother and children living and growing together in the closest relationship, intimately sharing in one another's lives, bound together by the strong bond of love. "Over all these virtues put on love, which binds the rest together and makes them perfect" (Col. 3:14). But the home needs the altar. If there is no altar, no self-sacrificing love or only a one-sided love, the family bonds are strained and often broken.

Someone has said, "A man travels the world over in search of what he needs and returns home to find it." Unfortunately, it often happens that people do not always find what they need and who they need at home. Many a child could agree with the rueful observation, "Be it ever so humble, there's nobody home." And perhaps there is a lot of truth in the wisecrack that the best way for a housewife to have a few minutes to herself at the close of the day is to start doing the dishes.

Self-sacrifice and kindness are essential for happy relations in a home. There is the story of the Kansas cyclone that took off the roof, picked up the bed with the husband and wife sleeping in it and gently set it down in the barnyard. The wife was weeping softly.

"Don't be scared," soothed the husband.

"I'm not," she replied, "I'm just so happy. It's the first time in twenty-five years that we've been out together."

The extent to which marriage, home and family life have degenerated is serious and alarming. Moralists, psychologists and marriage guidance counselors deplore it, books written by "experts" offer solutions and advice, but the divorce rate climbs higher and broken homes multiply.

Brutal pain is often inflicted in a divorce, and in general those who suffer most are the children. A divorcee wrote recently: "My daughter says she doesn't have a family, only a mother. She wants a daddy and brothers and sisters and a crazy, noisy family dinner hour. My heart saddens. I want those good feelings for her. Something is missing. I am missing the satisfaction of a life unfolding according to plan, ordained by God. Permanence is gone. So is security."

It is easy to be doctrinaire and to oversimplify, but much wisdom, patience and love are needed to untangle complicated and intimate human relationships. However, it is just as easy to go to the opposite extreme and represent marital happiness as something complex, difficult, and almost unattainable. In most cases, marriages can survive all kinds of hazards with just a little common sense, good naturedness, and the application of our Lord's "Golden Rule": "Treat others the way you would have them treat you..." (Mt. 7:12).

Unhappily, this rule and the simple lesson of self-sacrificing love which Christ taught for so long a time and with such unwearying patience is often forgotten, even by Christians.

The hidden years at Nazareth teach another lesson. They were an important part of God's plan of redemption. Even though they involved seemingly profitless, monotonous toil, a harsh, uninteresting existence and complete obscurity, yet they were as truly redemptive as His public ministry, His sufferings and His death on the cross. His humble submission and obedience to Mary and Joseph—"He went down with them and came to Nazareth, and was obedient to them" (Lk. 2:51)—were very precious in themselves and of great example to us. There was a reason for every aspect of Christ's life. Every moment of it was gathered up like the fragments remaining after the miraculous multiplication of the loaves. Nothing was wasted.

Each one of us lives a restricted and hidden-away existence, and if we could live our life over again, there would still be weary toil, monotony and frustration. But none of these things in our lives need be wasted. Work can be prayer. Even the most homely chores of everyday life can be offered to God as a prayer. "Whatever you do, whether in speech or in action, do it in the name of the Lord Jesus" (Col. 3:17). This can be our way of sharing in the great work of salvation.

> The trivial round, the common task,
> Will furnish all we need to ask:
> Room to deny ourselves, a road
> To bring us daily nearer God.

The hidden life emphasizes the importance of the supernatural. Christ loved concealment and deliberately sought it, even during the short years of His public ministry. He came as the Savior of mankind, but He did not just select a committee for an endless discussion of world problems, nor did He gather groups for "sensitivity sessions." He went alone into the desert wilderness to fast and pray for forty days and often He stole away to the lonely hillside to spend the night in prayer. This is the example He has left us. We must never forget those hidden sources of the supernatural; we must never undervalue the secret power of prayer and self-sacrifice.

Millions of ordinary people live lives of extraordinary beauty, courage and goodness because Jesus lives in them. They believe in this mysterious hidden presence within themselves simply because Christ told them of it:

> "Live on in me, as I do in you.
> No more than a branch can bear fruit of itself
> apart from the vine,
> can you bear fruit
> apart from me.
> I am the vine, you are the branches.
> He who lives in me and I in him,
> will produce abundantly,
> for apart from me you can do nothing" (Jn. 15:4-5).

The lives of Christian men and women may be spent in drab surroundings, in monotonous routine, in the performance of dull, unimportant tasks, in helpless pain and loneliness. Yet everyone who is united to our Lord has been born again and not only shares in the work of salvation, but is sanctified, is made a sharer in the divine nature, and can say with St. Paul, "The life I live now is not my own; Christ is living in me" (Gal. 2:20).

The Light of the World

An artist was painting a picture of a wintry twilight. A dark, gloomy house stood among leafless trees; there were patches of snow on the ground and puddles in a muddy country road. It was a cold, desolate scene, with an air of deep sadness and loneliness about it, until with a quick stroke of bright yellow paint, the artist put a lighted window in the house. The drab scene was transformed as if by magic into one of life and warmth, companionship and cheer.

Light is a symbol of the Godhead. God is spoken of as He "who dwells in unapproachable light" (1 Tm. 6:16), and Christ's coming on earth was predicted in terms of light:

> "A people living in darkness
> has seen a great light" (Mt. 4:16).

He described Himself as "...the light of the world" (Jn. 8:12).

A light gives guidance; it cheers and encourages. Christ is just such a light to us. His presence among us especially helps to dispel the gloom and the dark shadows caused by suffering and sorrow. An unusual happening recorded in the Gospel points to this.

In the heat of an August afternoon, Peter, James and John climb a high mountain with our Lord. The ascent takes them several hours, and when at last they reach the summit, the view before them ranges from the Syrian desert to the distant seacoast, uniting in one sweeping panorama the countries of Jew and Gentile.

Exhausted from their climb, the apostles rest and doze, until suddenly they awake to a remarkable spectacle. They see Christ completely changed—"transfigured." A mysterious, blinding light not only surrounds Him, but emanates from His transparent figure so that His clothes seem drenched with brightness. Although the three are dazzled and blinded, the sight strangely exhilarates them, and Peter voices their joy: "Lord, how good that we are here!" (Mt. 17:4)

Our Lord's transfiguration is not a meaningless event. It marked a turning point in His ministry. It coincided with the first intimations the apostles had of Christ's approaching sufferings and death. "From then on Jesus [the Messiah] started to indicate to his disciples that he must go to Jerusalem and suffer greatly there at the hands of the elders, the chief priests, and the scribes, and be put to death, and raised up on the third day" (Mt. 16:21).

It seems, then, that Christ meant His transfiguration to be a preparation and encouragement. It was as though He were saying, "Whatever happens to me, whatever humiliations and sufferings I shall undergo, and whatever sorrows shall darken the lives of all who follow me, remember always that I am God and I give you this glimpse of my supernatural glory and power so that you may never lose heart or doubt me."

No one on earth is exempt from suffering, and the colossal amount of pain in the world prevents many people from believing in God. The sad conclusion they have reached is that everything in the world has just happened by chance, things are to a great extent uncontrolled and we are all helpless victims of blind, unfeeling circumstances.

But this is no solution of the great problem of pain and sorrow. It ignores the presence in the world of much goodness and happiness, which outweigh grief and evil. And is it possible to believe that this amazing and intricately wrought world could have had no designer?

The only sensible answer is that an all-good and all-wise God made this world, but suffering is in it because of human sinfulness.

One always has the greatest compassion for those who suffer, and doubly sad is the lot of those who cease to believe in God because of their sufferings. Sorrow and pain darken our lives, but without belief in God, the darkness is unrelieved and impenetrable. This is unnatural: we are not meant to be creatures of such darkness.

Tromso in Norway is north of the Arctic Circle and its 40,000 inhabitants live two months of each year without seeing the sun. In this polar blackness, people become difficult to live with: they are edgy, sour and fretful. The whole city is said to slow down, the work capacity is reduced and there are complaints of tiredness. The mentally unstable may easily slip over the edge into mental disturbance; but even the emotionally healthy feel restless, fearful, and become preoccupied with thoughts of death. Everyone longs for the light. It is not natural for people to live in perpetual darkness.

Philosophical speculations about suffering are of little practical help since suffering is a deep mystery, even to the Christian. Christ is God, yet He deliberately chose to suffer every conceivable mental and bodily anguish. He is our answer to the question of pain. He is the Light of a world darkened by sorrow and suffering. He has not promised us immunity from pain and grief, but He has assured us He will give us courage and endurance. "Come to me, all you who are weary and find life burdensome, and I will refresh you" (Mt. 11:28).

There are times in our lives when we have to bear some unavoidable suffering, perplexity, loneliness and weariness. It seems no use then to try to be reasonable and logical. All we can do is to have a childlike trust in God. If we reason at all, we shall be rather like a little child who has to adapt itself to an unusual and frightening situation. Let us suppose the child has been taken suddenly ill and is rushed to the hospital, accompanied by its father. The child's mind might reason like this: "Here I am in this odd, frightening place, surrounded by strange people. I am in pain and afraid. I don't know what is going to happen to me, but my daddy is here with me. I know him and I can trust in him, so everything will be all right."

This may seem an over-simplification, but it is a truth of our Christian Faith that our dear Lord wants us to become as little children. He wants us at all times, but especially when we suffer, to have an unbounded trust in Him. He wants us to be like Job.

> "Slay me though he might, I will wait for him..." (Jb. 13:15).

Job had tried to find some explanation of his sufferings, but he failed, and his only relief was in acceptance and in complete trust in God.

We, too, have no other alternative but trust in God, because to do otherwise is to condemn ourselves to a darkness far worse than the blackness of a long polar night—the darkness of bitterness, resentment and despair.

To know that Christ suffered is light in darkness. It is to experience a mysterious spiritual joy and to have a deeper understanding and love of God, because then we begin to realize that sufferings are not just the unlucky accidents of life, nor are they meant solely to be a punishment or a deterrent. Like those of Christ, our sufferings can be creative and lead to newness of life. Their purpose may be only dimly glimpsed, but it is there. "Even now I find my joy in the suffering I endure for you," says St. Paul. "In my own flesh I fill up what is lacking in the sufferings of Christ for the sake of his body, the church" (Col. 1:24).

This is not escapism. We are comforted and encouraged as the three apostles were at Christ's transfiguration. Our faith and hope are strengthened; we persevere patiently with our prayers and our ordinary life and duties. And we trust in God.

"The Lord is my light and my salvation;
whom should I fear?" (Ps. 27:1)
"Even though I walk in the dark valley
I fear no evil; for you are at my side..." (Ps. 23:4).

One Who Cares

It has been said that fear is the origin of religion. It was supposedly fear of the unknown that led primitive man to invent a supreme Power and Deity; fear of punishment, pain and misfortune that led him to appease and placate this Being by worship; fear of death that led him to invent a life after death. Thus was religion born of fear and ignorance, according to this theory, and this accounts for the widespread decline of religion in our enlightened age.

It all sounds quite plausible, but it is not true. Was there ever such an age of fear as that in which we now live? And if, as it is alleged, fear is the basis of religion, then religion should now be flourishing.

Fear does have some part to play in religion. We always have some awe and respect for anyone who is greater than we are. God would not be God if we did not have some reverential fear of Him. When Christ calmed the storm for the panic-stricken apostles, the Gospel says, "Filled with fear and admiration, they said to one another, 'What sort of man can this be who commands even the winds and the sea and they obey him?'" (Lk. 8:25)

Once, when Christ drove evil spirits out of a man, his fellow townsmen were "seized with fear" (Mk. 5:15) and begged our Lord to leave their district. It was fear of Him that made His enemies act violently. The reason for our religiously indifferent age is its lack of a real awareness of God.

Fear is a healthy instinct provided it is kept under control, like any other of our instincts. But the truth is that God, in His relationship with mankind, has always revealed Himself as a God of love, as One who is a loving Father, as One who is to be loved. "Therefore you shall love the Lord, your God..." (Mk. 12:30). In pagan religions, fear of God predominated because they lacked this revelation of love. Even among the people of the Old Testament days, this revelation was not fully realized. The Jewish people had such a reverential fear of God that they hardly dared pronounce His name. Our Lord came to give that full assurance for which mankind hungered: the certain knowledge that God loves each human being He has created.

One of the images or symbols that Christ used to convey this truth was that of the shepherd.

"I am the good shepherd;
the good shepherd lays down his life for the sheep....
I am the good shepherd.
I know my sheep
and my sheep know me... (Jn. 10:11, 14).

This description was quite clear to our Lord's hearers. They understood that a shepherd is one who guides, protects and cares. The early Christians treasured this symbol; in paintings on the walls of the catacombs, Christ is depicted as a young shepherd. And still to this day, this image of God is one of the best-loved we have, although perhaps it has become sentimentalized.

One thing in it we may tend to overlook is that a shepherd is one who suffers, even dies, for his flock. This is the most important element in the image because suffering and sacrifice are sure signs of true love and devotion.

In an English churchyard there is a memorial to several shepherds who all died in one day when they went out on the moors to rescue sheep in a blizzard. And in Palestine, some years ago, a shepherd between Tiberius and Thabor fought three Bedouin bandits until he was killed by their knives and died among the sheep he was defending.

In the time of Christ, being a shepherd was a seven-day-a-week job in which the sheep came first and last, all the time. The Palestinian shepherd led the sheep from place to place for food and water, but he also went ahead so as to be the first to meet any danger. At night he slept across the threshold of the fold, still on guard.

Even now, being a shepherd is not an enviable job. Sheep are so vulnerable—they have nothing with which to fight or defend themselves. They are so helpless—if a sheep falls on its back and is left there, it will die because it cannot get to its feet without help. If it gets sick, it hides itself away somewhere. Probably of all God's creatures, sheep seem the most stupid.

A shepherd once told of a barn being set on fire by lightning. Sheep-cake had been stored there and the barn was still smoldering when an old ewe smelled the cake and led the whole flock to the red-hot food. The sheep went moping around for weeks afterwards, but the shepherd said they would behave the same way if it happened again the following week.

To us, sheep look alike, but the shepherd knows each one—the fussy ones, the lazy and clumsy, the bad-tempered and obstinate, the greedy, and the lamb-stealers who are not content with their own lambs. He is under no illusions about them. He knows their stupidity and cunning, their timidity and ingratitude. Yet there is something about sheep that arouses such care and love on the part of shepherds, and such patience, loyalty and devotion. Perhaps it is the very helplessness of the sheep.

Our dear Lord declared Himself to be the Good Shepherd. He wants us to see Him as the One who cares, loves, protects and provides for us. He knows each one of us so well, our different personalities, our oddities and potentialities:

"I know my sheep
and my sheep know me..." (Jn. 10:14).

He wants us to know Him, to know that He loves us in spite of our stupidities and weaknesses. He wants us to be so sure of His compassionate love of us that we will in all circumstances wholeheartedly trust in Him.

A bishop once told of visiting an elderly lady when he was a small boy. On the wall of a room in her house hung a painting of a large eye and beneath it the text, "You, O God, see me." Noticing his fascinated, frightened stare, the lady hastened to explain: "It doesn't mean that God is always watching to find fault with you. It means God loves you so much that He cannot take His eyes off you."

Again and again we must affirm our trust in God's love of us. May we submit ourselves completely to His guidance and protection.

"The Lord is my shepherd; I shall not want.
He guides me in right paths....
Even though I walk in the dark valley
  I fear no evil; for you are at my side
With your rod and your staff
  that give me courage.
Only goodness and kindness follow me
  all the days of my life" (Ps. 23:1, 3, 4, 6).

Look at This Heart

One of life's many tragedies is unreturned love. It has been the pathetic theme of many a play and novel. In real life, too, it frequently happens that a person loves someone, and the love is not returned. This is often the cause of a broken marriage, and there are many people whose old age is saddened because they are unloved and unwanted. Many good parents today ask themselves in bewilderment, "Where did I go wrong with my children?" They gave them good example and a good upbringing, but the children became selfish, wayward and even vicious. These parents share the bitterness of the sorrowing King Lear: "How sharper than a serpent's tooth it is to have a thankless child!"

Unreturned love is a divine, as well as a human tragedy. This was the great grief Christ Himself experienced.

"To his own he came,

Yet his own did not accept him" (Jn. 1:11)

is a description of His whole life. The thought of rejection by His own was with Him always. "He will be delivered up to the Gentiles" (Lk. 18:32). It was a thought that marred the joy of the Last Supper:

"I assure you, one of you is about to betray me" (Mt. 26:21). Even Pilate was mystified: "It is your own people and the chief priests who have handed you over to me. What have you done?" (Jn. 18:35)

The revelation of the Sacred Heart is a reminder that Christ's followers have not changed. His love is repaid with coldness and ingratitude. "Behold this heart which has so loved men and is so little loved in return." Christ portraying Himself as the Good Shepherd gave us a symbol of His love. But with the Sacred Heart He puts before us an emblem that has, perhaps, an even more profound meaning for us. He reveals God's unreturned love and makes a plea for reparation.

Nowadays, devotion to the Sacred Heart has declined, and many Catholics regard it as sentimental and unreal. It may therefore be interesting to note that the English martyrs of the sixteenth century honored the Sacred Heart as part of their devotion to the Five Wounds of our Lord.

In a cell on the second floor of the Salt Tower in the Tower of London can be seen a drawing of the Sacred Heart with a wound in it, carved into the stone by the martyr Henry Walpole. Martyrs are not sentimental.

Devotion to the Sacred Heart does not only mean that we pay special honor to the heart of Christ. An employer is sometimes said to "hire hands," or sailors at sea to get the order "all hands on deck," and it is understood that the whole person is being referred to. Similarly, the heart is a vital organ of the body and in this case it refers to the whole loving Person of Christ.

Scientists have always been fascinated by the mechanical perfection of the heart and by its prodigious activity, sending some six quarts of blood coursing through the arteries and veins of the body at a rapid flow. But the wonder of the heart does not just lie in its physical construction. It is a part of the body that is in close sympathy with our inner life. In hope and joy the heart beats freely; in grief, its movement seems heavy and slow; in anger and fear, it is quick and violent; in affection, it is steady and peaceful.

The Sacred Heart is indeed a well-chosen symbol of love, but we should not overlook the fact that the revelation is of a heart wounded and pierced by ingratitude and coldness. It might help us to understand this better if we recall the particular form that devotion to the Sacred Heart has taken.

A monthly remembrance on the First Fridays was requested by our Lord. We can understand why a Friday was chosen for this special remembrance and reparation, since it was on a Friday that Christ gave the great sign of His love by offering Himself in sacrifice for our redemption. Is there, however, any significance in the choice of the First Friday of every month? There seems to be some reason to think so, because Scripture scholars tell us there is evidence that Good Friday itself was indeed a First Friday—the fourteenth Nisan in the year of Christ's death.

According to the Jewish method of reckoning time, the legal day began after sundown. This means that our Lord instituted the Eucharist and the priesthood, underwent His hour of agony in the Garden of Gethsemani (the first Holy Hour), and died on the cross, at which time His heart was pierced—all on a First Friday.

In view of this, it is most fitting that the form taken by devotion to the Sacred Heart has been Eucharistic—Holy Hours, Masses and Communions

You Cannot Hold Back the Dawn

Most of us like to hear a success story, not necessarily because we want to escape from the mediocrity and monotony of everyday life, but because we are strongly convinced that this is how things ought to be—that ultimately all obstacles should be overcome and that life itself should end happily.

Truth is often stranger than fiction and real life contains many remarkable success stories, not least among them being that of Madame E. Schumann-Heink. Extreme poverty shadowed her childhood but she wanted to become a singer. She struggled through years of study and training only to be told that she would never make a career as a singer.

She married, but her husband was a wastrel and eventually left her with three children and a pile of debts which she tried to pay off until the struggle became too much for her. Living at starvation level, she fell ill, and almost demented with worry and despair, she resolved to kill her children and then to commit suicide. Only the entreaties of her eldest child prevented her.

This was for her the darkest hour before the dawn, which when it came, was indeed a wonderful dawn. A few years later she was a world-famous singer with the Opera Houses of Berlin, London and New York competing for her favors. Literally, success sprang from failure, because she herself declared that the tragedies of her life had enriched her singing. A mysterious quality, a blending of understanding and tenderness, had come into her voice which thrilled and captivated the hearts of millions of listeners.

The most remarkable success story ever known in history and one that has had worldwide effects and implications is the story of Christ's resurrection. His death on Calvary seemed to have been the tragic end of our Lord's life-story. His enemies also thought that Calvary was the end. "Let's see him come down from that cross and then we will believe in him" (Mt. 27:42). When He remained on the cross, they thought they had triumphed. "He saved others but he cannot save himself!" (Mt. 27:42).

For the shocked and sorrowing disciples, it was a time of dreadful darkness. They were utterly disillusioned. Christ had failed them; evil had triumphed over good; their hopes died when Christ died.

But they were all mistaken. Calvary was not the end. It had been the darkest hour before the dawn, and when the dawn came, it was the most brilliant our darkened world has ever seen—the dawn of the first Easter Day.

When our Lord began His ministry of teaching, people demanded proofs and signs. "Unless you people see signs and wonders, you do not believe" (Jn. 4:48). He not only promised them a sign, but He said that the sign He would give them would be His resurrection. Christ's resurrection is the great sign for all mankind, the sign of encouragement and hope, the sign of life and immortality arising out of death, the sign of goodness triumphing over evil and of success springing from apparent failure.

But what kind of sign is our Lord's resurrection? Is it no more than a kind of symbol? Did His resurrection actually take place? Simeon said of Christ that He was destined to be a sign that would be contradicted. Even today, the old attacks are still being made against the reality of our Lord's resurrection. And they are still shown to be wrong.

An eminent lawyer once said that if he were offered the choice of two briefs, the first to disprove the resurrection and the second to defend it, he would choose to defend it because that would be much easier to do.

The *Acts of the Apostles* opens with a simple statement: "In the time after his suffering he showed them in many convincing ways that he was alive..." (Acts 1:3). St. Paul lists some of the proofs. "He was seen by Cephas, then by the Twelve. After that he was seen by five hundred brothers at once, most of whom are still alive, although some have fallen asleep. Next he was seen by James; then by all the apostles. Last of all he was seen by me, as one born out of the normal course" (1 Cor. 15:5-8). It is most improbable that all these people could have been mistaken. It would be ridiculous to hold that they were all excitable, neurotic individuals. Moreover, the change which took place in the broken and dispirited company of the disciples is only explicable on the assumption that their belief was based not on fancy, but on fact.

Our Lord had openly foretold His resurrection, thus giving His enemies the opportunity to take every precaution to prevent any deception. He kept His wound-marks as proofs of His identity. In Rembrandt's picture of the supper at Emmaus, the hands of the Stranger stretched out upon the table show the print of the nails. They are the proof that doubting Thomas demands, and they are the proof that the Christ who lives is the Christ who died.

The Gospel descriptions of the resurrection are so vivid and confident that it is obvious the writers are referring to an event that was still fresh in the minds of intelligent men. And always there is that unaffected air of peace and tranquillity that speaks of the calm after the storm, rest and achievement after struggle and strife. Life is greatly changed, but many of the familiar relationships are resumed; there are meals together, conversation, instructions, and even a miracle.

The apostles proclaimed the truth of the resurrection fearlessly and with conviction. Writing to the Corinthians, St. Paul declared bluntly that if Christ were not risen from the dead, then the Gospel was worthless and they were still in their sins.

The existence of the Church and its survival through the centuries is proof of the reality of Christ's resurrection. The Catholic Church knows all about times of storm and darkness. It has gone through those periods when its enemies thought the end had come and when even the faithful must have doubted our Lord's promise to be with His Church all days. St. Augustine had every reason to fear the worst when Rome fell to the barbarians and the ages of struggle began. The dawn was a long time in coming, but eventually it did come. The Middle Ages that followed were to be known as the "ages of faith."

Injury to the Church, however, is always more grievous when the wounds are inflicted by those within the Church itself. Jansenism, a heresy which originated from the writings of a bishop, caused widespread harm to souls over a long period. Although it disregarded the supernatural order, it was upheld by three universities and by men of great learning. It was condemned again and again by successive Popes, but some bishops tried to prevent the condemnation.

An emperor enforced the heresy and by his order, divorce was permitted in his realm and Catholic customs such as confession, frequent Communion, processions and the veneration of the saints ceased. The world watched in amazement as it spread through many countries. A feature of this heresy was the crafty proceedings of its adherents, who stayed in the Church without renouncing their errors.

Yet again the darkness passed and the dawn came. The truth prevailed, the heresy waned and the Church lives on. And so it has happened time and time again; darkness and dawn, defeat and new life. It is happening now. Old heresies keep reappearing in new disguises. It will continue to happen in the years still to come. But we take heart because of the great sign that has been given us. "The Church," said Monsignor Knox, "has survived a hundred crucifixions by a hundred resurrections."

Someone once described an unforgettable incident in a visit to Palestine. It was Easter and he wished to be present at a sunrise service that was being held at the garden tomb, so he spent most of the night there. He was restless and could not sleep, and the night seemed endless. Fretfully, he turned to the Christian Arab who was his guide: "Will the night never end?"

In the candlelight, the calm face of the Arab rebuked him: "Never fear, my friend, the day will come. You cannot hold back the dawn."

Our Lord's resurrection is a sign for each one of us. If He had not died and risen again, we should never have known for certain the measure of God's love and mercy. There would have been no light for the people who walked in darkness because the breath and shadow of the grave would have clung to human existence. It is because He died and rose and lives that He is able to save us and make us share in a glorious life after death. "If we have been united with him through likeness to his death, so shall we be through a like resurrection" (Rom. 6:5).

Storms and trials darken everyone's life. The saints were not exempt. St. John of the Cross wrote at length about "the dark night of the soul." But the dawn always comes. "You cannot hold back the dawn." It came for Christ and His followers; it has come repeatedly for His Church; and if we but wait patiently and trustfully, it will come for each one of us.

"On the first day of the week, at dawn, the women came to the tomb bringing the spices they had prepared. They found the stone rolled back from the tomb..." (Lk. 24:1-2). Easter is for our encouragement. It is the day the Lord Himself has made, the great sign He has given us. Whatever horrors and evils may darken the world, whatever sufferings of mind or body may torture mankind, we must always remember that because of the certain sign we have been given, these things are of the night. A dark and terrifying night it may be, but "you cannot hold back the dawn."

The night passes and the dawn comes.

"At nightfall, weeping enters in,
but with the dawn, rejoicing" (Ps. 30:6).

Christ Was Heaven to Them

The *Acts of the Apostles* gives us a picture of Christ's disciples gazing upwards in perplexity when our Lord ascended to heaven. Angels then appeared and reprimanded them: "Men of Galilee, why do you stand here looking up at the skies?" (Acts 1:11) In a sense, people have been doing this since the human race began; they have been perplexed and have wondered what lies beyond this life, whether there is a life after death, and if so, what it is like. Human beings are the only creatures who know they will one day die and who worry about it. An animal is not tormented by any such perplexities; it is satisfied with its present existence.

We are always seeking happiness, permanent happiness; we are made this way. Often we seek it wrongly, and never do we possess it completely or permanently. Nor do material things, like wealth and fame, satisfy our cravings.

The brilliant Frenchman, Talleyrand, was the right-hand man of kings and emperors. He had just about every material comfort and pleasure the heart of man could desire; yet on his eighty-third birthday he wrote, "Eighty-three years of life are now gone, with no result but a great weariness, physical and moral, a profound sense of discouragement with regard to the future, and disgust for the past."

Christ spoke often of heaven as eternal life—words that at first sight are not very enlightening. Eternity in itself is not greatly attractive. Mathusala lived to be nearly a thousand years old, but he is not an inspiring figure of history. It is not duration of years that counts, but how we live. The Greek word translated as "eternal" does not imply duration only. Literally, it means "of an age" and so it points to life on another plane, a life not subject to time but above time; a life lived in other conditions than those of earth—conditions that are beyond the grasp of our imagination and comprehension. "Eye has not seen, ear has not heard..." (1 Cor. 2:9).

We pray that our dead may have eternal rest, but even the word "rest" can mislead us. It does not mean the inactivity of the soul after death, as though heaven were an endless sleep of oblivion. Rest is not always sleep. It can be relaxing activity. A factory hand or an office worker often gets rest from working at some hobby, or from games and sports. Heaven is, in our Lord's own words, "eternal life" and life cannot be static; it is dynamic—growth, movement and development. Christ said,

"My Father is at work until now,
and I am at work as well" (Jn. 5:17).

"Why do you stand here looking up at the skies?" (Acts 1:11) In spite of all our wondering and speculating, we are not much the wiser about heaven. Perhaps it is better for us if, instead of looking up to heaven, we simply look at our Lord. "Eternal life is this: to know you, the only true God, and him whom you have sent..." (Jn. 17:3).

Christ was heaven to His disciples. Some people have strong personalities and can profoundly influence and change others. The Gospels show us how our Lord completely revolutionized the lives of all kinds of different people.

People living in the time of Christ had their fears just as we have, but they were reassured by Him because He spoke with authority. He did not say, "Come to me all you who labor and are heavily burdened and I *think* I may be able to help you...." As surely as He healed their bodies, He mysteriously heartened and strengthened them in spirit. It gave them peace and happiness just to be with Him. "At the sight of the Lord the disciples rejoiced" (Jn. 20:20).

When He spoke of an eternity of happiness, they knew it was not mere wishful thinking to believe in Him. He spoke with authority and conviction.

> "In my Father's house there are many dwelling places;
> otherwise, how could I have told you
> that I was going to prepare a place for you?" (Jn. 14:2)

Not only the apostles and disciples, but also the early Christian Church became deeply imbued with a spirit of childlike trust regarding death and the after-life. The catacombs, those ancient underground burial places in Rome, give plenty of evidence of this. The inscriptions on the tombs of the Christians are unlike the melancholy pagan epitaphs. They are confident and hopeful: *Vivas in Deo*, "Live in God," and *In pace Christi*, "In the peace of Christ." There are no sad farewells, and the words "rest" and "sleep" are everywhere: "Gemella sleeps in peace." Expressions of affection abound: "To Aurelia Petronilla, sweetest daughter"; "Sweet Simplicius, live in eternity."

A guide to the catacombs was once asked what was his own chief impression of the catacombs. He replied without hesitation: "It is the atmosphere of utter faith and complete trust...I sometimes think that the world today, with its widespread materialism, is much like the Roman world of centuries ago. When I go down into the catacombs, I am in touch with a faith that could move mountains."

Years ago, we used to have public devotions for a happy death. It is surely a great grace and we should pray for it. Especially at night, before going to sleep, we can have the habit of commending ourselves to our Lord. "...into your hands I commend my spirit" (Lk. 23:46).

Sleep resembles death. Shakespeare called sleep the "counterfeit of death." To him it was both mysterious and sacred, and the enormity of Macbeth's crime lay in his slaying his victim while he slept: "Macbeth doth murder sleep...therefore Macbeth no more shall sleep."

If, before dropping off to sleep each night, we let our mind dwell gratefully and trustfully on our Lord, we shall be preparing for the happy death we pray to be given.

"Then let the weary body
A little while repose;
The last thought be of Jesus
Before the eyelids close."

He Keeps His Promises

Jonathan Swift once passed the cynical remark, "Promises and pie crusts are made to be broken." Certainly, the human record for fidelity to promises is not a good one. We are only too familiar with the type of politician who at election time makes glib promises that never seem to materialize. People make very solemn promises when they are married, priests when they are ordained, but such is the frailty of human nature that not even these are held sacred. St. Peter made a magnificent promise, but only a few hours later broke it. None of us can throw stones, because we all have our pitiful infidelities.

There are, of course, many instances of promises made and faithfully kept. Countless men and women have been loyal to their vows and promises even if their praises have been unsung.

A curious example of fidelity to a promise is the case of Andrew Carnegie, the multimillionaire. He was born in a two-room cottage in Dunfermline, Scotland. His father ran a weaving business in the tiny attic of their home. His mother worked sixteen hours a day, and Carnegie adored her. At twenty-two, he promised her he would never marry as long as she lived, and he did not marry until thirty years later, when she died. He often used to say to her,

"Mother, I am going to be rich some day so that you can have silk dresses and servants and a carriage of your own." He kept this promise, too.

We need promises. They are the foundation upon which we build our faith, hope and love. Religion is based upon promises, the steadfast promises renewed again and again, that God is faithful to those who love Him and that He will bless and reward all who in turn remain faithful to Him.

The ancient people of Israel believed that they had received a solemn promise from God. They called it a covenant, and this idea of a covenant is basic to the whole of the Old Testament. The covenant means that God graciously entered into a special relationship with them: He would be their God and they would be His people. The condition of the covenant was that the people should obey and serve the law of God. The law was read to them and the people responded, "All that the Lord has said, we will heed and do" (Ex. 24:7).

They were not always obedient. Time after time they defected, but although they abused God's goodness and deprived themselves of His help and protection, God never abandoned them. He kept His part of the covenant. Most noteworthy in all their long history was their deliverance from the cruel Egyptian oppression and their journey through the wilderness to the Promised Land. Ever afterwards they kept a special remembrance day—the feast of the Passover.

Our Lord was Himself the fulfillment of promises and He made many wonderful promises. He promised His followers His abiding presence and peace, forgiveness of their sins and Himself as food. He promised that whoever ate His flesh would live forever. He promised that He would comfort and strengthen all who came with their burdens to Him, and that He would give us His truth and guidance.

These and other promises were all condensed into the great event of the Last Supper. It was a renewal of the old and everlasting Covenant, but it was also a new Covenant, because He sealed it with His own blood and He gave not just a symbol or His word, but Himself, as a pledge of His fidelity. "...this is my body" (Mt. 26:26).

The Eucharist is both sacrifice and sacrament. It is the most perfect act of worship, the perpetuation of Christ's supreme sacrifice of atonement. Hilaire Belloc, the writer, said that of all he had read about St. Louis, nothing delighted him more than the French king's custom of going to Mass daily, even when he was with his army on the Crusades.

Belloc himself spoke of one of the satisfactions he got from attending Mass. He said that in the Mass you do all that the human race needs to do and has done through many ages. "There is the sacred and separate enclosure, the altar, the priest in his vestments, the set ritual...and all that our nature cries out for in the matter of worship."

It is quite wrong to suppose that the Mass is only a meal or banquet uniting members of a community together. Immolation and expiation are among the chief reasons for the ancient ritual act of sacrifice, but a meal does not convey any idea of oblation. In a sacrifice, a subordinate offers homage and submission, but a meal is usually among equals. At the Last Supper, our Lord did not say, "Let us eat...." but, "Take this and eat it..." (Mt. 26:26).

The Communion in the Mass is the completion of the sacrificial offering. While always preserving deep respect for the sacredness of Christ's own sacrifice, we should not overlook this other aspect—that the Mass is a joyous Eucharistic celebration. The partaking of a meal should be a joyous occasion. It is usually a sign of friendship. In the East, it is an assurance of help and protection; when an Arab breaks bread with a stranger, it means that he will not harm him.

The early Christians rejoiced that in the Mass, or as they termed it "the breaking of bread" (Acts 2:42), they had God's promise and assurance of His help and protection. Christ predicted that if He were lifted up He would draw all men to Himself. The Mass has always exercized a mysterious but powerful influence upon mankind. Our attitude towards the Mass and Holy Communion should be one of joyous desire. We ought not to come to Mass merely through routine and habit, or even from a sense of duty only. Least of all should we be complacent and condescending.

Our Lord said, "Blest are you who hunger..." (Lk. 6:20). In her Magnificat, Mary rejoiced because, "The hungry he has given every good thing..." (Lk. 1:53). St. Paul exhorted the Corinthians to "Set your hearts on spiritual gifts" (1 Cor. 14:1). Cervantes said, "Hunger is the best sauce." A spiritual hunger is the best disposition for Mass and Communion. We should approach them eagerly and often, full of joy and desire, hungry for our Lord; hungry for His presence, His peace and His strength; hungry for greater love, courage and trust; hungry for His assurances and the fulfillment of His promises; hungry for

"God's bread [which] comes down from heaven and gives life to the world" (Jn. 6:33).

Only God can satisfy the hunger that is in every human heart.

The difference between goodness and the other things for which men and women live is that only goodness satisfies; all other things breed discontent. A man who lives for success, never reaches the heights he wants to reach, and every success makes him ambitious for more. God is the source of all goodness and only in Him can our desires find fulfillment and rest. He has promised us this satisfaction and He keeps His ancient promise to all who are faithful to Him.

"I will not violate my covenant;
the promise of my lips I will not alter"
(Ps. 89:35).

His promise and His presence are lasting.

The Mystery of Faith

The world of nature is full of wonders, but perhaps the greatest wonder is that we take so many of them for granted. As an example, suppose you were given a small box or receptacle made out of lime and filled with a thick, glutinous substance. Suppose you were told to keep it in a warm place, and that in a few weeks' time it would transform itself into a watch, already running perfectly, complete with dial, hands, mainspring, and every tiny rivet and screw needed.

You would laugh at such an absurdity! Nevertheless, it is a fact that something even more wonderful is a commonplace happening of nature. A bird's egg is an oval receptacle formed of lime (the shell), and filled with a shapeless, almost colorless substance. Kept in a suitable temperature, it will be transformed, not into a piece of mechanism, but into a living, sentient bird.

Within the fragile shell are formed the bones of legs, wings and spinal column; each tiny, brittle bone is beautifully fashioned, polished smooth as ivory and knit together with utmost precision, according to a distinct plan. Flesh and skin clothe the entire skeleton, while throughout the whole, run slender channels carrying blood from one extremity to the other. Heart, eyes, pointed beak, lungs, throat, and wings are all in that miniature universe.

Here indeed is wonder and mystery! But this is only a small mystery among the countless wonders around us—yes, and within us. For what is human life, thought, imagination and memory? What is sleep, and what are dreams?

Why then, are we so hesitant about accepting the mysteries of religion? Why act as if mystery were a new experience? Should we not expect to find God's ways and dealings with us even more remarkable and mysterious than the mysteries of nature?

Of all God's wonders, none can be more mysterious than His presence in the Eucharist, which we daily proclaim to be the "Mystery of Faith." Yet despite Its mystery, it is difficult to understand how any Christian could doubt the real presence of Christ in the Eucharist, or question that mysterious transformation of bread and wine into the living body and blood of Christ. Our Lord taught it so clearly that there can be no mistaking His meaning and purpose.

What could be more simply stated than those words of institution, "This is my body.... This is the cup of my blood"? Long before the Last Supper, Christ had taught the doctrine of the Eucharist:

"I myself am the living bread
come down from heaven.
...my flesh is real food
and my blood real drink" (Jn. 6:51, 55).

And He prefaced this teaching with the miracle of the multiplication of the loaves.

It is worthwhile considering this miracle, for it can help us to a better understanding of Christ's real presence in the Eucharist. How did our Lord feed the thousands with just five loaves? There are only two ways in which He could have done it. Either He could have distributed the five loaves and then created from nothing some thousands of new loaves; or He could, without creating a single fresh loaf, have caused the loaves to be miraculously present in many places. This last seems to be what He did. St. John distinctly says, "Jesus then took the loaves of bread, gave thanks, and passed them around..." (Jn. 6:11). Afterwards, St. John tells us, "...they gathered twelve baskets full of pieces left over by those who had been fed with the *five barley loaves*" (Jn. 6:13). In other words, it was the presence of the loaves that was multiplied. Each of the loaves was made present at one and the same time, in many different places, and eaten by the vast crowd.

This may not lessen the mystery, but it helps us to understand the reality of Christ's presence in the Eucharist. If two priests in different places offer Mass at the same time, this does not mean that two different persons of Christ become present at the consecration. It is not the Person but the presence that is multiplied. The same sacred body is present in two places. When several hundred people receive Communion, each receives the self-same body of Christ which is present in several hundred places. In a somewhat similar, but even more real and wonderful way, just as a speech is heard over the radio by millions of people, or as the sun makes its presence felt in many different places, so Christ makes Himself really present all over the world.

However deeply we may delve into this mystery, the Eucharist will always be as it was in the beginning, a "hard saying," a mystery and a challenge to our faith. In this it is merely an extension of that greater mystery, the mystery of divine love. But it is also a proof of God's love of us, because love always desires union.

Prayer Is Power

One day in 1926, the coal-fired freighter *Ripley Castle* steamed into Cape Town from America. Among the stokers was a young man named Tony Madison, and it was his first trip to sea. In the tropics, work in the stokehold was unbearable. On duty one night, and almost suffocated by steam and fumes, he was near fainting and was sent on deck to get some air. Eyes streaming and half-dazed, he slumped down at the ship's side and fell overboard.

The water quickly revived him and he shouted wildly, but soon the ship's lights were moving steadily away from him. A faint hope that he would be missed and a search would be made for him kept him swimming with a slow breaststroke in the wake of the ship.

It was not until an hour later that the alarm, "Man overboard" was raised, and the captain swung the ship round and steamed back at full speed. Madison scarcely realized what was happening. Utterly exhausted, he saw a ship's lights and called out with the last ounce of his strength, but he was unconscious when he was dragged aboard the ship's lifeboat.

Later, the chief officer added further details to the story. He was a deeply religious man and used to hold prayer and Bible study meetings for the men.

Just before this event, Madison had wished to consult him, but the chief officer was busy at the time and had promised to see him later. When he learned that Madison was lost overboard, he was filled with remorse. The young man had needed his help and he had failed him. He prayed as he had never prayed before, pleading desperately as he thought of the sharks and that vast wilderness of an ocean.

When the ship had steamed back for nearly an hour, it slowed and the chief officer, straining eyes and ears, thought he heard a faint cry. He himself took charge of the boat that was lowered. He prayed all the harder, believing now that God was hearing his prayers. Steering the boat at random into the darkness, he shone his torch and saw Madison's head in the water.

Prayer is a mysterious power. It cannot be otherwise, for it is the creature reaching out to the infinite and invisible God, the Creator of all things.

"Prayer is a force as real as terrestrial gravity," says Dr. Alexis Carrel, twice winner of the Nobel Prize. "As a physician, I have seen men, after all other therapy has failed, lifted out of disease and melancholy by the serene effort of prayer. It is the only power in the world that seems to overcome the so-called 'laws of nature.'"

There must be many people who regard prayer as a formalized routine of words, a last resort for the desperate, or a childish asking for material things. How sad that prayer should be so misunderstood and undervalued! It is somewhat like describing rain as something that fills the birdbath in the garden. Properly understood, prayer is a mature activity; it is a need of our higher faculties. Only in prayer do we find a satisfaction for our spiritual aspirations.

The daughter of Karl Marx was one day talking to a friend. "I was brought up without any religion. I do not believe in God." Then she added a little wistfully,

"But recently in an old German book I came across a prayer, and if the God of that prayer exists, I think I could believe in Him." Asked what the prayer was, the daughter of Karl Marx repeated slowly in German the Lord's Prayer.

How can we prevent our prayers from becoming a mere formalized routine of words and make them instead into a source of strength and power? First, we must believe in prayer. The Jews were always known to be a praying people. They had an old saying, "Prayer, the weapon of the mouth, is mighty." Nor did they doubt that God listened to the prayer of all His children.

"You who hear prayers.
To you all flesh must come..." (Ps. 65:2-3).

"Do you believe this?" our Lord asked Martha just before He raised her brother Lazarus to life (Jn. 11:26). "Are you confident I can do this?" He queried the two blind men who had begged for their sight to be restored (Mt. 9:28). Christ tells us we need unlimited faith when we pray. "You will receive all that you pray for, provided you have faith" (Mt. 21:22). We ought to begin our prayers with an act of faith in God's presence and goodness. We dishonor Him and weaken our prayers if we think they go unheeded, or are not answered in some way which is according to His will and purpose.

The next important thing about prayer is *to want something*. This does not mean that we should pray only in times of need, or that "wanting something" only applies to bodily needs. But it does mean that if we come to prayer complacently and self-sufficiently, or from routine and a sense of duty, then our prayers will be unreal and halfhearted, boring and ineffective.

"The hungry he has given every good thing,
while the rich he has sent empty away"
(Luke 1:53).

It is right, of course, to pray for bodily needs. Christ Himself teaches us to do so: "Give us each day our daily bread" (Lk. 11:3). But He also reminds us that we do not live by bread alone. Indeed we have many deep spiritual wants: we need God's forgiveness, guidance and protection from all evil; we need His peace and happiness; we need greater knowledge and love of Him; we need to praise Him, to thank Him, and to seek the wider extension of His love, His kingdom on earth.

How can we awaken these spiritual wants in ourselves? It is not a matter of artificially creating them. Reading the Scriptures or the books of wise and saintly writers will remind us of them. Like Shakespeare, we should see "books in the running brooks, sermons in stones and good in everything." To saints like Francis of Assisi, all creation mirrored God. The greater our realization of God, the more conscious we shall be of our poverty and needs.

It has been said that if you want something badly and set your mind on getting it, more often than not, you will get what you want. Our Lord has told us we should never be discouraged with our prayers. He once described a man being awakened late at night by a neighbor who had unexpected visitors and had no bread in his house. It is a very humorous and human situation.

Houses of the poor in the time of Christ consisted often of just a single room, at one end of which was a raised platform; here the parents and children slept. The lower part of the room had an earthen floor and was occupied by the animals—the donkey, goats and chickens. The door would be bolted by a long wooden pole passed through iron rings.

When all are settled down for the night, imagine the disturbance and upheaval caused by the sleepy master of the house having to pick his way in the darkness over the sleeping children, among the frightened animals, and then finally having to wrestle with the door fastenings. But the late caller refused to go away, and for the sake of peace, the owner of the house had to get up and give him what he wanted.

The great essentials of prayer are faith, confidence and submission. We must believe that God hears us, that He wants to give us what is best for us, and that He is able to grant whatever we request. The intensity of our prayer and the wholeheartedness of our submission are the measure of our faith and love. This is how Christ Himself prayed in the Garden of Gethsemani. "Father...not my will, but yours be done" (Lk. 22:42). And the Gospel adds: "In his anguish, he prayed with all the greater intensity" (Lk. 22:44).

The Presence of the Holy Spirit

Nature usually performs its greatest works in a silent, mysterious way. The magic dawn of each new day emerges silently out of the gloom and darkness of the night. In the springtime of each year, the life hidden away in the roots of trees and shrubs, stirs and silently spreads through the leafless branches until even the tiniest twig is clothed with the fresh green of buds and leaves. In our own bodies there is growth and development as the blood noiselessly passes through arteries and veins, building up bones, muscles and flesh, molecule by molecule, fiber by fiber.

Our Lord has told us there is an even more hidden and mysterious presence and power that dwells within us and gently influences us—the presence and power of the Holy Spirit.

"The wind blows where it will.
You hear the sound it makes
but you do not know where it comes from,
or where it goes.
So it is with everyone begotten of the Spirit" (Jn. 3:8).

The activity of the Spirit is creative and life-giving, but it is silent and secret. It is inevitable that mystery should shroud the Holy Spirit.

More than two thousand years ago, Aristotle was asking how the mind is "attached" to the body. It is a question that is still unanswered. If our own nature of part-body and part-spirit is so mysterious, we cannot expect anything else but that impenetrable mystery should surround the Holy Spirit. Yet it is surely significant that one of the earliest beliefs of primitive people was of spirit-life and of the indwelling of spirit.

When the Israelite King Saul disobeyed God, the Bible says: "The spirit of the Lord had departed from Saul..." (1 Sm. 16:14). He remained king, but he was a changed man, subject to moods of deepening depression, until finally in despair, he committed suicide. His successor, David, had a better reign, but it was spoiled by his sins of adultery and murder. As though remembering Saul's melancholy fate, he prays contritely:

"Your holy spirit take not from me.
Give me back the joy of your salvation,
and a willing spirit sustain in me" (Ps. 51:13-14).

The prophets were the mouthpieces of the Holy Spirit. We hear Ezekiel saying in awe: "Spirit entered into me and I heard the one who was speaking" (Ez. 2:2). Isaiah, peering through several centuries prophesied:

"A shoot shall sprout from the stump of Jesse,
and from his roots a bud shall blossom.
The spirit of the Lord shall rest upon him:
a spirit of wisdom and of understanding,
A spirit of counsel and of strength,
a spirit of knowledge and of fear of the Lord"
(Is. 11:1-2).

Joel predicted that the messianic age would witness a great outpouring of the Holy Spirit:

"Then afterward I will pour out
my spirit upon all mankind.
Your sons and daughters shall prophesy,
your old men shall dream dreams,
your young men shall see visions;
Even upon the servants and the handmaids,
in those days, I will pour out my spirit" (Jl. 3:1, 2).

And when those days did at last come, a young Jewish virgin maiden was startled by an angel appearing to her, telling her she had been chosen to be the mother of the Messiah. When she asked how this could be possible in view of her vowed virginity, she was told: "The Holy Spirit will come upon you..." (Lk. 1:35).

Elizabeth was filled with the Holy Spirit and proclaimed the praises of Mary and her Child. John the Baptist, the last of all the prophets, gave his testimony: "I saw the Spirit descend.... The one who sent me to baptize with water told me, 'When you see the Spirit descend and rest on someone, it is he who is to baptize with the Holy Spirit'" (Jn. 1:32, 33).

At the beginning of His ministry, Christ was led by the Spirit into the desert to pray and fast, and here He had a mysterious encounter with the spirit of evil—Satan. The casting out of evil spirits was later a part of His ministry.

Jesus ended His ministry with the promise of the Holy Spirit. At the Last Supper, He spoke with tender concern:

"If you love me
and obey the commands I give you,

I will ask the Father
and he will give another Paraclete—
to be with you always:
the Spirit of truth,
whom the world cannot accept,
since it neither sees him nor recognizes him;
but you can recognize him
because he remains with you
and will be within you" (Jn. 14:15-17).

Read the early history of the infant Church, the *Acts of the Apostles*, and you will see the fulfillment of the ancient prophecies and of Christ's promise. This was the time when the essential goodness of the Old Law was purified and preserved and when the spirit of the pagan world was challenged. It was a time when God's creative Spirit seized upon and activated human souls as never before nor since, and when the fragile growth of the Christian Faith was nourished and strengthened.

Read, too, the letters of St. Paul, and you will see how utterly he is possessed and influenced by the Holy Spirit, and how often he speaks of the Spirit's presence and power. "The Spirit we have received is not the world's spirit but God's Spirit..." (1 Cor. 2:12). "Are you not aware that you are the temple of God, and that the Spirit of God dwells in you?" (1 Cor. 3:16)

The lives of saints, martyrs, and courageous Christian men and women of every land and era are proof of the creative, strengthening and guiding power of the Holy Spirit. They are evidence that we have truly received the Spirit that comes from God (cf. 1 Cor. 2:12).

Jonasz Stern was a Polish painter imprisoned by the Nazis. One day he was lined up with others before a firing squad, but was only wounded. He fell under the bodies of his companions, and after dark, crept out and escaped. Later, he gave an exhibition of his paintings, and they were all pleasant, smiling landscapes. None of them showed any trace of the inhuman treatment he had endured. We speak of the triumph of the human spirit, but how much of this triumph is due to the revivifying power of the Holy Spirit?

For all of us there are occasions when we need the help, guidance and encouragement of the Holy Spirit. There are the times when our faith is tested. St. Paul says that only through the Holy Spirit can we say, "Jesus is the Lord." Often we are tempted to anger, hatred or pride and resentment—can we not picture to ourselves Christ's disapproval? "You know not of what spirit you are," He seems to tell us. And sometimes we are weary, discouraged, or afraid, and we need to beg,

> "Your holy spirit take not from me.
> Give me back the joy of your salvation,
> and a willing spirit sustain in me"
> (Ps. 51:13-14).

Living by the Spirit is the theme of St. Paul's writings. How can we do this? The scholarly Cardinal Mercier was Primate of Belgium during the first World War, a time for him of great anxiety and anguish, yet he was known to be always remarkably composed and cheerful. He recommended a practice of the presence of the Holy Spirit. It should be possible for everyone.

For five minutes every day, try to shut out from your mind and imagination the sights and sounds of the world around you, especially all fears and anxieties. Withdraw into the sanctuary of your baptized soul, the temple of the Holy Spirit. Surrender yourself completely to the presence and power of the Holy Spirit. Repeat this simple prayer, "I will be still and rest in You, O Holy Spirit of peace within me."

Keep on affirming your belief and trust. You can think of St. Paul's description of what he calls the "fruits" of the Holy Spirit: charity, joy, peace, patience, mildness, faith. Or you need think only of the words, "I will be still and rest in You." Say them at different times throughout the day. Say them at night before going to sleep, or if you are worried or afraid as you lie awake at night.

By this constant repetition you will be practicing the presence of the Holy Spirit whom we tend to forget and neglect. You will be letting the realization of this wonderful presence go deep into your consciousness and you will be building up a great reserve of spiritual strength, joy and peace upon which to draw in time of need.

The action of the Holy Spirit is usually secret and gentle. Our attitude should be one of loving trust and desire: "Come Holy Spirit...I will be still and rest in You."

A Great Sign Appeared...

Thursday, February 11, 1858, was a cold, dismal day, and three poorly-clad and ill-nourished children were gathering firewood in the countryside near a small town in the south of France. A stream in the meadow blocked their way and two of the children waded across it. The freezing water made them cry out with pain.

The eldest of the three girls suffered from asthma and feared that the cold would bring on an attack if she followed her companions. She tried to make a causeway with stones but failed. Childlike, the others mocked her efforts and then ran off, leaving her alone.

She had decided to wade through the stream when she was startled by a sudden loud, rustling sound, like a gust of wind. It was strange because everything remained perfectly motionless. She had stooped to remove her stockings when the sound came again, and now she noticed that in front of her, at a little distance up the rock face of a cliff, the leafless branches of a bush were tossing violently in the still air. And then suddenly, in a niche near the bush, the figure of a woman appeared.

The fourteen-year-old child was afraid. She wanted to call after her companions; she thought she must be mistaken; she rubbed her eyes and looked again. The figure was still there, and now it was smiling at her and beckoning her to come nearer. Instead, the frightened child took out her rosary and knelt to pray. She tried to make the sign of the cross, but somehow could not, until the figure showed her how to make it slowly and reverently. She was afraid no longer, and her shrewd peasant eyes closely observed the mysterious stranger.

The figure stood against a background of golden light. It was the figure of a woman dressed in white with a blue sash around her waist and a white veil over her head and shoulders. She was young and not very tall; she was beautiful beyond description, and she was very much alive. After a little while, the lady bowed, smiled and disappeared. The bright light lingered, then slowly faded, and once more the recess was empty and the rocks cold and bare.

Thus began the apparitions at Lourdes, the eighteen memorable appearances of our Lady to Bernadette, the little peasant girl. The story is well known, but because of its charm and simplicity, it is never dulled by repetition. But what is the position of Lourdes in this scientific and skeptical age? Is Lourdes authentic, and can we know whether or not the apparitions are true?

The world today may be skeptical, but in many ways it is credulous and gullible. Freakish movements flourish. Nothing causes surprise or suspicion.

In December of 1971, it was disclosed that a man in England had claimed to be an associate member of the Royal Institute of British Architects, and he had obtained a key job with a London firm of architects. He had held the job for some time, but when asked to make some drawings for an important project in London, he had produced work that was said to be useless rubbish. The truth about him then came out. He had had very little schooling, had earned a record for dishonesty and was a deserter from the Army. It was in the Army that he had picked up his very meager knowledge of architecture. Yet nothing had ever been done to check his qualifications.

The Church has always exercized the greatest caution with regard to people who claimed to have divine visions or messages. It was only after long and careful scrutiny that the Church finally declared the apparitions of Lourdes to be authentic.

Our Lord Himself warned us about false prophets, the sheep in wolves' clothing, those who would deceive even the saints among us. He told us of a test we could make in such mysterious and important matters. "You will know them by their deeds," He said (Mt. 7:16). It is a simple but effective way of knowing prophet from pretender, truth from falsity.

Many books have been written about Lourdes, but the best proof of its authenticity and meaning comes from considering some of the few words spoken by our Lady. "Will you do me the favor of coming here every day for two weeks?" The Mother of God asks a favor of an illiterate peasant child!

"I only knew the rosary," said the uneducated Bernadette, humbly. God chooses the lowly. Long centuries ago, the call from God had come to Moses and David, who were shepherds, and it had come to Mary, who was herself a lowly Jewish maiden.

It is never God's way to force our human mind or will. Gabriel, the great archangel, waited for Mary to consent to be the Mother of God. Mary too, shows perfect respect and courtesy with Bernadette. Belloc rightly observed:

Of courtesy, it is much less
Than courage of heart or holiness;
Yet in my walks it seems to me
The grace of God is in courtesy.

"Drink of the spring and wash in it." Bernadette had turned toward the stream, but our Lady pointed to the ground in front of the cave. The child obediently scraped the soil until a trickle of muddy water appeared—the beginning of the spring with its ceaseless flow of water and wonders.

This Lourdes water is ordinary water without any healing properties. The sick, some of them with open cancerous wounds, bathe in it, but there has never been a single case of transferred infection. Samples of the bath water have been chemically analyzed, and have been found to be heavily infested by malignant germs, but the Lourdes water has rendered these germs so harmless that the water may be drunk safely.

Christ appealed to His miracles as proof of His divinity.

"Even though you put no faith in me,
put faith in these works" (Jn. 10:38).

The miracles of Lourdes, the humanly unaccountable cures of every kind of organic disease, set the seal of divine approval and authenticity on Lourdes. Mary intercedes for a suffering and unbelieving world, just as long ago at Cana in Galilee she made her compassionate request: "They have no more wine" (Jn. 2:3).

"I wish a chapel to be built and the people to come here in procession." In a world that is all too familiar with hostile and often trivial demonstrations, and in the Catholic world which has mostly abandoned its outdoor processions, millions of people still make their way to Lourdes every year. Greater numbers visit the hundred-year-old shrine than ever before. Modern travel facilities are partly responsible, but Lourdes itself exercises a powerful worldwide attraction. Many of the great pilgrimages are made up of poor people who manage to get to Lourdes only through sacrifice and hardship.

The sick are there in thousands, a good number of them in the advanced stages of their illness. Many people, however, do not come seeking only bodily favors. Miracles do still take place, but those who have had long experience of Lourdes say that miracles are not spoken about as much as in earlier days. The concern is more about faith, prayer, and the supernatural.

Moreover, while it is still a great Marian shrine where our Lady is cherished and honored, Lourdes is also a great international Eucharistic center. Every day during the pilgrimage season, hundreds of Masses are offered and thousands of Communions received; there is exposition of the Blessed Sacrament; every afternoon brings its pageantry and procession in honor of the Eucharist. Just to witness the faith and fervor of the vast crowd and to hear the heartfelt prayers—"Lord we adore you; Lord we trust in you; Lord, that I may see"—is to be taken back to Gospel times. This is the great miracle of Lourdes: our Lady leads twentieth-century men and women to her divine Son.

"Do penance...pray for sinners." The Gospel message to a pagan world is the same as our Lady's message to Bernadette. "You will all come to the same end unless you reform" (Lk. 13:3). Disease, poverty, war, injustice and cruelty are all evils, but sin is the root-cause of them; sin is the greatest of evils.

"I do not promise to make you happy here, but in the next life." While others benefited, Bernadette suffered ill-health and trials all her life. Our Lady herself suffered so much that she is called the Queen of Martyrs. The way of the cross is for many of us the way to eternal happiness.

"I am the Immaculate Conception." This is the climax of the apparitions. Bernadette said that the words were spoken with profound humility. They are words from heaven confirming the supernatural beauty and power of a creature made perfect by God. They are words reminding us that God's purpose in choosing Mary was that she might cooperate with Christ in the salvation of mankind. "A great sign appeared in the sky, a woman clothed with the sun,... and on her head a crown of twelve stars" (Rev. 12:1).

At about the same time as the Lourdes apparitions took place, two books were published that had a catastrophic effect upon the world. Charles Darwin wrote about his theory of evolution and Karl Marx propounded his doctrine of dialectical materialism from which came Communism. It was the beginning of a new era. The wheels of industry, science and technology were turning towards an earthly paradise of progress and achievement for all mankind. The world would be "freed at last from the shackles of religious superstitions."

"You can tell a tree by its fruit" (Mt. 7:20). We know only too well how bitter have been the fruits of these two theories. If people believe they are no more than evolved apes, can they be blamed for turning the world into a jungle? If Communists believe that religion is opium and there is no God or an after-life, can they be blamed if mass-murder, lies and injustices are to them perfectly legitimate means to any perverse end?

Lourdes must be seen against this sinister background. It is a portent of hope, a reminder of the ancient prediction of the Scriptures that evil cannot prevail against Mary. As in the Gospels, the words she spoke at Lourdes are few and brief, but her message is urgent and clear. Let us heed it. We are called to share in the salvation of the world. We must repent and pray.

The words of St. Bernadette are also encouraging and should bring us closer to Mary. Someone asked the child whether our Lady looked only at her during the apparitions. "Oh no," she replied, "she looked at different people, and sometimes she smiled affectionately, as though greeting a special friend."

Mother of Us All

In the early part of World War II, a young Hungarian Jewish writer who had joined the French army was taken prisoner. It was vitally necessary for him to conceal his identity because he had attacked the Nazi regime in his writings. A French soldier captured with him suggested that the Hungarian should share his name and identity. They would probably be sent to different prison camps, and two men with the same name would pass unnoticed. He gave the Hungarian his identity disc and some letters from his mother.

"If anyone questions your identity, just show these letters," he advised. Later, the Hungarian read the letters. The writer, he thought, was probably some peasant woman with a wrinkled face, roughened hands, and a shawl over her head, but the letters might have been written by his own mother. "Take care of yourself, my son.... Wrap yourself up warm.... I hope you get plenty to eat.... Don't forget your prayers! ...God bless you and bring you safely home."

All mothers, all over the world and in all ages, have written the same kind of letters to their children.

The centuries-old belief that Mary, the Mother of God, is also the mother of us all, is an immensely consoling belief. What could be more consoling than to know that someone close enough to God as to be His Mother is also close enough to us as to be our own mother? And like all mothers—indeed far more than any mother—she is patient and loving, always deeply concerned about us, sometimes anxious about our welfare and happiness; above all, she is a mother who is able to help us in our times of pain, loneliness and temptation.

But is all this really true? What proof is there that God's Mother is also our mother?

It is not mere sentiment but sound reasoning and theology that have, from the early days of Christianity, recognized Mary's all-embracing motherhood. As soon as Christians clearly understood that Christ was truly God, they realized that Mary must be the Mother of God. To deny her this title would be a denial of the truth that God became man. Christianity means that we are the brothers of Christ. God shared our nature that we might share His. From this it is a logical step to the belief that the Mother of God is the mother of us all.

Origen, a writer of the early Christian days, said, "By this title we are Mary's sons, because we are her own Son's brothers." A reverential affection for Mary is the identifying mark of the Christian. Cardinal Newman declared that those groups which depart from the Catholic tradition of devotion to Mary eventually lose faith in the divinity of Christ. Always, those who are devoted to Mary draw closer to Christ.

But our belief in Mary's motherhood of mankind does not rest on mere human reasoning. To support it are the very conclusive words Christ spoke on the cross: "Woman, there is your son" (Jn. 19:26). On the surface, the words might seem to mean nothing more than that our Lord was making material provision for His mother. But why, when every word must have cost Him pain, did Christ go on to say, "There is your mother"? (Jn. 19:27). St. John, to whom the words were spoken, already had a mother and there was little material help that Mary could give to John. The meaning of this solemn utterance can only be found at a deeper level. Christ was speaking of a new motherhood that was being established.

This is more clearly indicated when we understand that St. John writes very differently from the other Gospel writers. He does not just report incidents and facts, but gives their inner meaning and purpose. He is always concerned with the deeper significance of events. And so, for instance, he does not merely report the miracle of the loaves as do the other writers, but he links this happening with the profound theology of Christ's teaching on the Eucharist. Similarly, he links the miracle of Lazarus being raised to life with Christ's teaching on His own and our resurrection to life after death.

And so St. John understands these words from the cross as having a special significance. They are not to be taken in isolation. He understands them as marking the termination of Christ's ministry, because immediately after them he says, "After that, Jesus realizing that everything was now finished, said to fulfill the Scripture..." (Jn. 19:28). What had been the beginning of our Lord's ministry? St. John had already recorded it—the miracle at Cana, in which Mary had played a prominent part and at which time Jesus had addressed her in a similar way: "Woman" (Jn. 2:4). And what had been one of the earliest Scriptural prophecies but that there would be enmity between the "Woman" and Satan? This enmity in which Satan would be ultimately vanquished was fully established when Christ's Mother became the mother of mankind.

The word "enmity" has an awesome reality about it, especially when it refers to the malevolent satanic powers of evil and hatred. In this life we are in enemy-occupied territory. "Wars," said a writer of antiquity, "are hated by mothers." In wartime, mothers of soldiers live in an agony of suspense, anxiety and desolation.

"Woman, behold your son." Mary received her great charge and duty at a time of intense realism and suffering. She cannot have regarded lightly that solemnly-given commission, nor has she ever done so through the succeeding ages. Lourdes and Fatima show her increasing concern for mankind in our own age. Devotion to Mary our blessed Mother, far from being something merely pretty and sentimental, is a realistic requisite for us all.

More than ever before we need the help and protection of the rosary and we need to cultivate towards Mary a close, personal relationship of child-like love and confidence. This should not be difficult. She is indeed like all mothers but her perfection, position and power of intercession make her a mother beyond all comparison.

We Take Her as Our Own

In the *Acts of the Apostles* we are told that Mary, the Mother of Jesus, was with the disciples gathered in prayer after Christ's ascension into heaven. She has been with them ever since. She is the Mother of God and the Mother of His Church. She is the new Eve and the mother of mankind.

We must not let her exalted position be a hindrance in our relationship with Mary, who is the mother of each one of us. Some of the titles we give her imply an aloofness—Mother of God, tower of ivory, house of gold, and Immaculate Conception. Mary is unique, but she is one of us; she is a human being. She is not just a lot of titles, however glorious and true. She is a human person.

Just as we say "Our Father" because by adoption we are truly God's children, and just as we call Jesus "our Lord" because by Baptism we are His brethren and co-heirs with Him, so we call Mary "our Lady" because she is of our nature, and because God, the maker of all motherhood and of a mother's love and instincts, has made her our mother. Like the apostle John at Calvary, we take her as "our own"!

We have, then, a real and a close relationship with Mary. What relationship could be closer than that between a good mother and her children? Chesterton wrote of motherhood: "...hidden in every home, a voice that sings about the house, a nurse that scares the nightmares off, a mother, nearer than a spouse."

The first requirement of any mother is that she rear her children, caring for them and supplying their vital needs. The instinct to do this is strong, even in wild animals.

It is chiefly our spiritual needs that are the concern of Mary, our heavenly mother. She fosters and strengthens our relationship with God. She helps us to pray.

Broadly speaking, prayer is divided into praise and petition. The Gospels are full of instances of these two kinds of prayer. How does our Lady encourage, guide and aid us with these two basic forms of prayer? She gives us her rosary and the Hail Mary!

First, there is praise. Praise is not the false coin of flattery. We give praise where it is due. Each decade of the rosary reminds us of something worthy of praise in the joys, sufferings and triumphs of Christ and His Mother told in the Gospel story of our redemption. We shall enrich our prayers and pray the rosary better if we use each decade as a special reminder and reason for praise. The first part of each "Hail Mary" will express our praise, "Blessed art thou amongst women and blessed is the fruit of thy womb, Jesus."

Next, there is the prayer of petition. Sometimes a mother is asked, "Which of your children do you love the most?" It is a foolish question because a good mother loves all her children equally, but one mother once gave a lovely answer:

"I love most the one who is sick until he is better, and I love most the one who is away until he comes home again."

When we were very small and were hurt or frightened, we ran to our mother as fast as our little legs could carry us, confident that she would help us in our need. But even grown men—soldiers fatally wounded in battle—have groaned in their agony the name of "mother."

Mary is the merciful mother of all mankind and we come to her, conscious of our needs and trusting in her power to help us in all of them. The rosary will rid us of our feeling of self-sufficiency because each decade reminds us of some virtue, some grace or help which we desperately need: a stronger faith, greater humility and submission, more trust, gratitude and forgiveness. We are confident because we remember Cana in Galilee when she merely said to her Son, "They have no more wine" (Jn. 2:3). And so we say, "Holy Mary, Mother of God, pray for us sinners now, and at the hour of our death."

Truly, she is "our" Lady, "our" mother. She is the "voice that sings about the house." She sets us singing the praises of her Son. The rosary is everybody's Psalter. Unfortunately, it is often sadly misunderstood. Some object to it, quoting Christ's words, "In your prayer do not rattle on like the pagans. They think they will win a hearing by the sheer multiplication of words" (Mt. 6:7). But our Lord was condemning mechanical repetition here, not the prayer of a loving heart that seeks the presence of God to praise and thank Him continually. Used properly, the rosary can gladden and enrich our lives.

Mary is the "nurse who scares the nightmares off." She loves us because of our helplessness and especially at those times when existence can almost be called "nightmarish."

Someone once described the love of a good mother as "an abyss with forgiveness at the bottom." Mary is merciful, and therefore, she is "a mother, nearer than a spouse."

The Kingdom To Come

"Shangri-La" in James Hilton's novel, *Lost Horizon,* the remote and beautiful place where life approaches perfection, is perhaps a dream most of us cherish. St. Thomas More had such a dream when he dreamed up a perfect city and called it "Utopia." God has a dream, a plan for the world which He is still trying to establish, and He called it His kingdom.

This kingdom is the central message and proclamation of Christ's teaching. The word is mentioned over a hundred times in the Gospels. Our Lord tells us to pray that it may be established, and we must have made the petition "thy kingdom come" many thousands of times, perhaps without fully realizing its importance. What does it mean?

To avoid confusion, we should understand that the expressions "kingdom of God" and "kingdom of heaven" mean the same thing; the word heaven is sometimes substituted for that of God, because of the Jewish reverence for the holy name. It is also better to speak of the kingdom as the "kingship" or "reign" of God.

The phrase "the kingdom of God is at hand" means God is at the point of beginning His reign; the kingship, the royal power of God within the world is about to begin.

It is necessary that we should know about the common practice in Jewish literature and poetry of using what is called "parallelism," that is, the custom of saying everything twice. The same idea is expressed again in different words. Often the second part not only restates, but explains the first part. The Psalms have many examples:

"And he led forth his people with joy;
with shouts of joy his chosen ones" (Ps. 105:43);
"Let Israel be glad in their maker,
let the children of Zion rejoice in their king" (Ps. 149:2).

And so in the Lord's Prayer, two petitions appear close together and the second clarifies the first: "...thy kingdom come; thy will be done on earth as it is in heaven." The meaning is clear. To be in the kingdom of God and to do the will of God are the same thing. To be a member of the kingdom necessarily involves acceptance of God's will.

As soon as we see the kingdom in terms of the will of God, it becomes something real and practical. It is not something remote and dream-like—a Shangri-La or a Utopia. If God's will were carried out perfectly by all men and women, the world would become a heaven on earth.

But the kingdom, seen as the will of God, also becomes something personal. It is not something which first and foremost involves nations, peoples and countries. The kingdom of God is something which begins with me. The person prayed wisely who prayed, "Lord, revive Your Church, beginning with me." We should apply the petition in the Lord's Prayer primarily to ourselves.

It is obvious that the kingdom of God cannot be forced on anyone. It must "come." It is God's personal invitation to each of us to accept His will. Hence Jesus pictures it as a banquet to which the host issues invitations, and which the guests accept to their gain and glory, or refuse to their loss and shame.

If they do accept, then there must be observance —they must have on the customary wedding-feast garment, they must accept the laws and rules of their host, they must do God's will in all things. And so it is that the kingdom of God and repentance always go hand in hand. Anyone entering the kingdom must have that change of mind which makes him stop seeking his own will, and instead, accept God's will. "Seek first his kingship over you..." (Mt. 6:33).

This is not always easy. A strong, deeply-rooted instinct of our nature tends to make our own will, desires and inclinations the dominating and moving force in life.

Wealth makes entry into the kingdom very difficult, too. "It is easier for a camel to pass through a needle's eye than for a rich man to enter the kingdom of God" (Mk. 10:25). Our Lord is not saying that wealth prevents our entering into the kingdom, but that it makes it very difficult. Prosperity often makes people forget the kingdom, forget God.

More than anything else, an unforgiving spirit debars a person from the kingdom. Christ makes this quite clear in His parable of the unforgiving debtor. Anyone who has a grudge or a resentment against a fellow man would be out of place in the kingdom of love. A heart of hatred has automatically closed a door to the love of God.

The kingdom of God is worth any price and sacrifice. Jesus describes it as both a treasure hidden in a field and a pearl of great price. The finder gives everything he has to become the owner of such riches. Sometimes it happens that we have to sacrifice position, comfort, even some close personal relationship in order to enter the kingdom. "Whoever loves father or mother...more than me is not worthy of me. He who will not take up his cross and come after me is not worthy of me" (Mt. 10:37, 38).

St. Thomas More, the English martyr, knew he had only to agree to the King's divorce and to his claim to be the Head of the Church in England, and he would have saved his life, remained the King's friend, retained his position as Lord Chancellor, and above all, kept the home and family he loved. Instead, he chose martyrdom. "I die the King's good servant, but God's first."

Does this mean that the kingdom is meant only for saints and martyrs? To counteract any such discouraging conclusion, we have Christ's assurance that God's kingdom is for all. People will come from the north and the south and the east and the west to sit down in the kingdom. There are no racial or class distinctions, no favored peoples or nations in God's universal kingdom.

Indeed our Lord emphasizes the fact that a childlike spirit is one of the essential conditions of entry into the kingdom. A child has two great qualities: humility and trust. They are the keys of heaven, and even Peter must use them. This is why the kingdom of God has the smallest and lowliest of beginnings; its growth is secret and like that of the mustard seed, the smallest of seeds.

The kingdom is within us; it is not anything spectacular. The little acts of self-conquest and kindness to others, the prayers and Holy Communions, the commonplace life which someone described as "so daily"—these bring about the growth of the

And He Was a Samaritan

More than any other class of people, the Samaritans seem to have been singled out by our Lord for kindly consideration. A Samaritan was the hero of Christ's great story about compassion. It was to a Samaritan woman that He spoke at great length and with loving concern at the well of Jacob, and He pointed out that the only grateful one among the ten cured lepers was a Samaritan. It seems that it was of them He was speaking when He told His disciples,

"Open your eyes and see!
The fields are shining for harvest!" (Jn. 4:35)

Who were the Samaritans? And why were they given such prominence and favored treatment by our Lord, especially since they were despised by official Judaism?

Originally, the Samaritans were Israelites who in the exile had been left behind in Samaria and had intermarried with the Assyrian invaders. After the fifty years of exile, the tribe of Judah returned from Babylon and were known in the future as Jews. When they began to rebuild the ruined Temple of Solomon in Jerusalem, the Samaritans offered to help, but the Jews refused their offer on the grounds that they were not now strictly Jewish.

The Samaritans never forgot nor forgave the insult. They set up a rival temple on Mount Garizim. Jews and Samaritans no longer had dealings with one another; indeed, the Jews regarded the Samaritans as unclean and always avoided contact with them. The Samaritan woman asked Christ, "'You are a Jew. How can you ask me, a Samaritan and a woman, for a drink?' (Recall that Jews have nothing to do with Samaritans.)" (Jn. 4:9). At the time of Christ, the age-old feud was as strong as ever. The Samaritans often waylaid Jewish travelers and ill-treated them.

What unpopularity and even hatred must our Lord have incurred among strict Jewish scribes and priests! Whenever He spoke kindly of Samaritans, He was going completely against popular feeling. Yet for all His kindness, He did not deny that they were schismatics.

> "You people worship what you do not understand," He said to the Samaritan woman;
> "While we understand what we worship;
> after all, salvation is from the Jews" (Jn. 4:22).

Is there any lesson to be drawn by us from our Lord's friendly and sympathetic attitude to this outcast people? Surely it is the all-important lesson of His compassionate love for us.

Compassion is defined as "sympathy for the distress of another, together with the desire to alleviate it." How often the words, "pity" or "compassion" occur in the Gospels! "At the sight of the crowds, his heart was moved with pity. They were lying prostrate from exhaustion, like sheep without a shepherd" (Mt. 9:36). Of a leper it is said: "Moved with pity, Jesus stretched out his hand, touched him, and said: 'Be cured'" (Mk. 1:41). Of the blind men: "Moved with compassion, Jesus touched their eyes" (Mt. 20:34). And of the widow woman of Naim: "The Lord was moved with pity upon seeing her" (Lk. 7:13).

The same sentiment is evident in our Lord's two greatest stories. In the story of the prodigal son we read: "While he was still a long way off, his father caught sight of him and was deeply moved. He ran out to meet him..." (Lk. 15:20). In the parable of the Good Samaritan, it is this stranger who shows compassion to the robber's victim: "[He] was moved to pity at the sight" (Lk. 10:33).

Twice Christ's heart was so touched with compassion that He broke down and wept. Always He has a boundless compassion for the poor, the diseased and the downtrodden. Though He never condones sin, He has such compassion and forgiveness for the repentant sinner that He is called "friend of sinners" (cf. Lk. 7:34).

In her Magnificat, our Lady twice praises the mercy of God and says it "is from age to age" (Lk. 1:50). St. Paul cries exultantly that we Christians are "vessels for mercy—which he [God] prepared for glory—I am speaking about us whom he called, not only from among the Jews, but from the Gentiles. As it says in the Book of Hosea: 'Those who were not my people I will call "my people," and those who were not loved I will call "Beloved"; in the very place where it was said to them, "You are not my people," they shall be called sons of the living God'" (Rom. 9:23-26).

Trust in God's mercy and compassion are the basis of the widely loved "Little Way" of St. Thérèse. "His infinite mercy is the quality that stands out in my life, and when I contemplate and adore His other perfections, it is against this background of mercy all the time.... Even if I had all the crimes possible on my conscience, I am sure that I should lose none of my confidence.

"Heartbroken with repentance, I would simply throw myself into my Savior's arms, for I know how much He loves the prodigal Son. I have heard what He said to Mary Magdalene, to the woman accused of adultery, and to the Samaritan woman. No one can make me frightened any more, because I know what to believe about His mercy and His love: I know that in the twinkling of an eye all those thousands of sins would be consumed as a drop of water cast into a blazing fire."

Hundreds of years ago, the writer of the Psalms asked a question that perhaps we, too, have sometimes asked:

"What is man that you should be mindful of him,
or the son of man that you should care for him?"
(Ps. 8:5)

Does God really love us? He who reads the secrets of the heart and knows how petty, selfish, conceited and spiteful we are—what can He see in us that is lovable?

"This man was a Samaritan" (Lk. 17:16). Christ is compassionate and He loves us more than a good mother loves her sick or ne'er-do-well child. He is more compassionate than a selfless, generous-hearted person who pities the underdog and the outcast.

Our Lord will reveal the secrets of His heart to us as He once did to a sinful Samaritan woman, "I who speak to you am he [the Christ]" (Jn. 4:26). He will receive us with gladness whenever we thank and praise Him.

"Give thanks to the Lord for he is good,
for his mercy endures forever" (Ps. 118:1).

And He will reward us, if for His sake, and like the good Samaritan, we have kindness and compassion for others.

As We Forgive

During one of Ireland's troubled periods of history, Joseph Brady was sentenced to death for having killed Burke, the permanent Under-Secretary. Brady refused to make his peace with God because he could not find it in his heart to forgive a man called Carey, who had informed on him. The chaplain of Montjoy Prison brought in many holy priests to pray with Brady to try to persuade him to forgive Carey. Brady's answer was always the same: "God Himself would not expect an Irish patriot to forgive an informer."

The day before the execution, a nun appeared at the prison gate and begged to be allowed to see the condemned man. Entering Brady's cell, the nun apologized for her intrusion, but said she had desperate need of help. As one about to face God, Brady would be the most likely man to give her some advice.

She explained that she hated a certain person with all her heart; it had become an obsession with her, and she now asked Brady if she should throw off her veil and leave the religious life. Brady replied without hesitation,

"For God's sake, Sister, don't do that. Try to forgive."

"Very well, Mr. Brady," the nun said, "I forgive you for killing Burke in Phoenix Park. He was my brother."

Brady asked her forgiveness, made his confession and received Holy Communion next morning before he was hanged.

Forgiveness of others, even our enemies, is one of the "hard sayings" of the Christian Faith. Christ teaches it, not as a counsel of perfection for the few, but as a commandment and an essential requirement of all His followers. He stresses the importance of forgiveness by telling us of the consequences of our failure to forgive others. Outside His parables, there are only three occasions when Christ explicitly speaks of the punishment of hell: when people fail to perform the works of mercy, such as feeding and clothing the poor, caring for the sick and imprisoned; when grown-ups corrupt little children; and whenever there is an unforgiving hatred of others.

Christ even condemns what some consider only slight infringements of the law of charity and brotherly love. He denounces all words of anger, ridicule and contempt: "Any man who uses abusive language toward his brother shall be answerable to the Sanhedrin, and if he holds him in contempt he risks the fires of Gehenna" (Mt. 5:22).

To be unforgiving is to perpetuate hatred, to harden ourselves in hatred. Hatred is a form of violence, and a violent act is an act that is contrary to the nature of a thing. Violence is destructive, and hatred is satanic. "Anyone who hates his brother is a murderer," says St. John (1 Jn. 3:15).

A famous psychologist has said that whenever someone hatefully shouts at another, "Go to the devil!" he is being more realistic than he thinks, because he is expressing the hidden desire to destroy someone.

Wholehearted forgiveness of those who have hurt, opposed, ridiculed, or insulted us, is one of the most difficult things in the world. We sometimes say, "I will forgive, but I can never forget; I can never trust him again." But this is not the forgiveness the father had for the prodigal son; it is not the forgiveness Christ prayed His enemies might receive from His Father. And it is not the kind of forgiveness we hope to have from God.

Christ emphasized that only as we forgive can we hope to be forgiven. "If you do not forgive others, neither will your Father forgive you" (Mt. 6:15). He taught us to pray, "forgive us our trespasses as we forgive those who trespass against us." St. John Chrysostom said that in his day there were many who suppressed this phrase in the Lord's prayer.

The parable of the unrelenting debtor makes it quite clear that an unforgiving person cannot hope for forgiveness. As we judge others, so we will be judged. In matters of mercy we will get what we give.

The inescapable truth is that the condition of forgiveness is the forgiving spirit. General Oglethorpe remarked to John Wesley, "I never forgive." Wesley answered, "Then I hope, sir, that you never sin." We can only have God's forgiveness when we are not only sorry for our sins, but have also a sincere desire to forsake them. If we are not prepared to show others the mercy we ask for ourselves, it is proof that there has been no real change of heart in us.

How can we learn forgiveness? First, we should try always to remember how easy it is to find fault and condemn others and at the same time to be quite blind to our own failings.

"I may have my faults," said a man having an argument with his wife, "but being wrong is not one of them." Christ said it was possible to see a speck of sawdust in someone's eye while a wooden beam was in our own.

We need to avert our attention from the injury done to us by recalling what was perhaps the more serious harm we ourselves may have done to others. This will humble us, calm our indignation, and make us want to have God's forgiveness.

Next, we ought to seek constantly to live in an atmosphere of charity and peace. There are occasions when we must disapprove and even be angry with injustice and cruelty. But we should take care to hate the sin and not the sinner, and if we have to correct others, then we must endeavor to do so with kindness and understanding. The prescription of St. Francis de Sales should not be forgotten: "An ounce of honey is more effective than a barrel of vinegar."

If we have quarreled or given offense, we should seek reconciliation quickly, for delay can only prolong and intensify the harm done. "The sun must not go down on your wrath" (Eph. 4:26). Our Lord seems to stress the need for quick reconciliation, "Leave your gift at the altar, go first to be reconciled with your brother, and then come and offer your gift (Mt. 5:24). More often than not, we shall find the other person coming to meet us half way.

Finally, we must never forget that prayer is an unfailing means of banishing all thoughts and feelings of enmity and hatred. Whenever we ask

God to forgive us our sins, we must beg Him to give us His spirit of forgiveness, and we must pray also for any who have injured us. If we want to be right with God, we must be right with others.

The old story of Leonardo da Vinci is probably more legend than fact, but it enshrines a great truth. It is said that when he was painting his famous picture of the Last Supper, he painted the portrait of an enemy as Judas Iscariot. But the face of our Lord would not come right. Then he forgave his enemy, painted out his portrait and substituted an imaginary figure. After that he had no further difficulty with Christ's face.

It will always be unalterably true that we are never closer to our Lord and more like Him, never more genuinely Christian than when we forgive our fellow men.

"This is how all will know you for my disciples: your love for one another" (Jn. 13:35).

I Confess

One morning in July, 1971, a man gave himself up to the police near his home. He confessed to having murdered a woman twenty-one years before. He said it had been preying on his mind, especially at night, and he was prepared to accept any punishment for his crime.

"The last twenty-one years of my life have been ruined," he said. "For two minutes of drunken temper or madness, I made my life a nightmare. Already I feel better. I can think with a conscience cleared of its terrible secret. I am at peace now. It's like being born again."

When the writer, G. K. Chesterton, was once asked why he became a Catholic, he replied, "To get rid of my sins." He was quite serious. He said that confession was God's way of re-making human beings; the absolved sinner becomes a new creation; he is once again an innocent child. "He may be old and gouty, but he is only five minutes old."

Confession means the soul is released from all its consciously stored-up sins. The burdens of guilt and remorse are lifted. It is therefore a necessity for mental and spiritual health. Unless sin is gotten rid of, sooner or later it produces harmful effects—a sense of hopelessness and despair. Unconfessed sin paralyzes further efforts; like suppressed steam, it is dangerous. It is not good to store up grief or any strong emotion. Shakespeare said:

"Give sorrow words; the grief that does not speak
Whispers the o'er fraught heart and bids it break."

Professor C. G. Jung, the internationally-famed psychologist, said that when prospective patients who were Catholics came to consult him, he sent them first to confession. However, confession, or the sacrament of Penance, is not just a psychiatric exercise. It is something more than the mere telling of our sins.

It is some relief to bring our sins out into the open, but we want more than this. We want our sins to be taken away and to be destroyed. We want to be assured of God's forgiveness. Christ knew of this need and when He was on earth, He Himself gave definite assurance of the forgiveness of sin. "To help you realize that the Son of Man has authority on earth to forgive sins..." (Mt. 9:6).

Our Lord understood that the more sincere a person's sorrow was, the more discouragement there would be over sin and the harder it would be for a soul to be convinced of having been forgiven. With His parables, He stressed the mercy of God. He Himself always encouraged the repentant sinner: "Have courage, son, your sins are forgiven" (Mt. 9:2). "Nor do I condemn you" (Jn. 8:11).

Christ gave His Church the power of forgiveness which He had exercised:

"If you forgive men's sins,
they are forgiven them" (Jn. 20:23).

He did not intend it to be used indiscriminately—a vague, general pronouncement of forgiveness that would hardly be worth having. It was a sacred trust; it was a power that had to be ministered according to justice, tempered by mercy, but in absolute sincerity:

"If you hold them bound,
they are held bound" (Jn. 20:23).

Should we go to confession frequently? The Lord's Prayer is meant to be a daily form of prayer and in it is a petition for the forgiveness of sin. However, frequent confession is frowned upon in some quarters nowadays, on the grounds that it may become mechanical and cease to be truly penitential. But habit and routine can make *any* spiritual exercise monotonous and boring. It is up to us to see to it that this does not happen.

The Vatican Council urged priests to be mindful of how much the sacrament of Penance contributes to developing the Christian life. It asks them to make themselves available to hear confessions. They are to exhort the faithful to approach the sacrament with a contrite heart. Frequent confession is a well-established Catholic tradition, and it must have many advantages.

People who live in slum conditions and a polluted atmosphere are often not conscious of the squalor and the smells. Those who rarely go to confession seem unable to remember any sins, even though they may be selfish, greedy, idle, conceited and uncharitable. Their conscience has become dulled and atrophied through lack of use. Confession purifies the conscience.

Being a sacrament, confession gives grace to the soul. This grace has a healing, restorative effect, and it builds up resistance against sin. Serious sins must always be confessed, but this does not mean that smaller sins can be taken lightly. Although they are not mortal wounds, they can account for the spread of apathy and carelessness over the soul, like a torpor.

Because of its sacramental character, confession not only takes away the guilt of sin, but also remits the temporal punishment more effectively than ordinary private acts of sorrow.

Since it is never easy even to acknowledge a mistake or to apologize to someone we have offended, confession, too, may be irksome. However, "confession is good for the soul," and some joy and gain always result from a humble confession. Every sincere confession is a renewal, a fresh start. We are all creatures of habit and we need to take stock of ourselves from time to time. If we do a thing once, it is always easier to do it the next time. Every evil act reinforces the evil tendency in our nature. "What is the use of running if you are on the wrong road?"

Spiritually, perhaps most of us have not even started walking. Frequent confession could act as a spur. We would be reminded of our sins of omission—the opportunities we did not always use, the gifts we neglected to employ in the best way, and the behavior that is dangerously like that of the servant in Christ's parable who did not use the one talent he had been given.

The confessions we make regularly may encourage others to follow our example. This is especially important where children are concerned. Assertions have recently been made that "preadolescent children are incapable of evaluation and therefore cannot be subjectively guilty of sin." This is absolute nonsense. A child knows at an early age when he has been naughty and offended his parents. He knows that it is wrong to steal, to disobey, to quarrel and to be greedy, selfish and cruel.

To deprive children of confession is to withhold grace from them and to remove an effective form of training for a healthy mental and moral outlook.

Someone has shrewdly observed that in one period of the Church's history there was a kind of phariseeism which discouraged people from frequent Communion on the grounds that they were not good enough. Now the situation is reversed, and people are dissuaded from confession because they are not bad enough!

Without being over-anxious and scrupulous, we must not let confession become mere routine. Prayerful reflection will always prevent this from happening. Moreover, there is no danger of becoming mechanical if our approach to confession is a personal one. Confession is a very personal sacrament. While the good of a sermon is diffused among many people, the forgiveness and the graces of the sacrament of Penance are concentrated upon an individual soul.

It is Christ's pardon and absolution we receive, so we must endeavor to see Him in this sacrament. May we try always to be deeply conscious of His infinite love and compassion, seeing Him as the Good Samaritan gently tending to our wounds, comforting and encouraging us, turning our sorrow into joy and giving us His peace.

Many non-Catholics spoke of Pope John as "good Pope John" and this is how he will be remembered in history. When he was in his eightieth year he wrote,

"During my whole life I have kept faithful to my practice of weekly confession. Several times during my life I have renewed my general confession." A few years previously he had said,

"There are two gates to paradise: innocence and penance. Which of us, poor frail creatures, can expect to find the first of these wide open? We may be sure of the other, however. Jesus passed through it, bearing His cross in atonement for our sins, and He invites us to follow Him. But following Him means doing penance, letting oneself be scourged, and scourging oneself a little, too."

Fulfillment

Self-realization and fulfillment are widely discussed at present, especially among young people who speak of wanting to know how to relate to others and to life. They seek to find their real identity and insist on "doing their own thing." This is perhaps not surprising, since modern life tends to become more urban, impersonal and stereotyped.

But the search for fulfillment is not something new. Throughout the whole of nature, a power urging all living organisms to some form of fulfillment can be observed. It is present even in plant life: creepers will move to a stake so that their tendrils may climb it; when a leading shoot of a young tree is cut off, the next highest branch alters its direction to take its place.

The urge for completion can be seen in the salmon that returns from the sea to fight its way up river in order to spawn and die in the very spot where it began life. It can be seen in the bird that builds its nest, rears its young, travels miles over land and sea to a warmer climate, and then returns in the spring to its place of origin.

The impulse to find fulfillment is even more marked in human beings. We all know the dissatisfaction of an unsolved problem, of a task that is not completed, of a story that has an unhappy ending

—or none at all. It seems a shame to us when a promising young person dies, and a great sin when those who are gifted waste their talents.

The force in us seeking fulfillment is indeed mysterious. We cannot find completion and self-realization in ourselves alone. Selfishness is destructive. To seek one's own will, pleasure and satisfaction only brings frustration. To use a familiar illustration: the snows of Mt. Hermon feed the Sea of Galilee and the Dead Sea. The former gets water and gives it, and so it is a place of fertility and beauty. The latter keeps its water, and so it is stagnant and desolate.

Giving is the only way to self-realization. Christ once said, "Give, and it shall be given to you.... For the measure you measure with will be measured back to you" (Lk. 6:38). We get what we give. The greatest human achievements have been brought about by the complete giving of dedicated men and women. In our everyday life we find that if we give consideration, kindness and help to others, we usually get the same from them in return.

Utterly selfish people have a warped character; they are not mature or grown-up. And they are not happy people. Those who keep everything for themselves are called misers—from the Latin word for miserable.

God has Himself set the pattern of giving before us. Not only is He "the giver of all good gifts" (cf. Jas. 1:17), but He has given Himself.

"God so loved the world
that He gave His only Son" (Jn. 3:16).

Christ gave Himself to us at the Last Supper: "This is my body which will be given up for you." This giving was completed on Calvary.

> "There is no greater love than this:
> to lay down one's life for one's friends" (Jn. 15:13).

In the Mass, Christ perpetuates this giving of Himself.

"Rings and jewels are not gifts," Emerson said, "but apologies for gifts. The only true gift is a portion of thyself." What can we give to God? Ourselves. A holy person once remarked, "We are not likely to be called upon to shed our life's blood for God. But let us give it to Him, drop by drop, in each little duty." Prayer, submission to God's will and our trust and confidence in Him are all a giving of a portion of ourselves.

Every time we turn promptly from temptation, every time we endure hardship or disappointment with patience, every time we make an act of self-denial, we give of ourselves. Finally, we give of ourselves when we have sympathy and compassion for others, when we care for their needs and spend ourselves in their service.

This giving of ourselves is the only way to happiness, fullness of life and true self-realization. "Whoever loses his life for my sake will find it" (Mt. 16:25). The growth of Christ in us, which is the Christian ideal, can only be accomplished by the continued giving of ourselves.

> "Unless the grain of wheat falls to the earth and dies,
> it remains just a grain of wheat.
> But if it dies,
> it produces much fruit" (Jn. 12:24).

The measure we give is the measure we get back. But a complete giving of ourselves is never easy.

We have strong and deeply-rooted, self-regarding instincts. We need the help of God's grace; we need prayer. St. Francis of Assisi had a prayer that expresses our need:

> "Divine Master, grant that I may not so much seek to be consoled as to console;
> to be understood as to understand;
> to be loved as to love;
> for it is in giving that we receive,
> it is in pardoning that we are pardoned,
> and it is in dying that we are born to eternal life."

St. Ignatius has a somewhat similar prayer:

"Take, O Lord, into Your hands my entire liberty. Receive my memory, my understanding and my will. All that I am and have, You have given to me; give me only Your love and Your grace. With these I am rich enough and I desire nothing more."

Empty Hands

There is a story of an Arab traveling through the desert and making camp at night. Being very tired, he was soon asleep, but he was awakened in the dark by movements and heavy breathing outside his tent. He lay still, alert and listening, and then he smiled and relaxed when he realized it was only one of his camels that had gotten loose. He knew he ought to get up and tether it, but he was very tired. It would soon go away and it would come to no harm, so the weary Arab drifted off to sleep again.

But the camel did not go away. Scenting food, it explored cautiously, thrusting its head through the tent's opening. Becoming bolder, it advanced a foot inside. Then suddenly rearing its head, it brought the tent down, tearing the flimsy canvas, scattering food and cooking utensils, and trampling upon the startled Arab.

It has been said that the spread of evil only requires that good people should do nothing. We hope that evil things will go away, or we sweep unsightly things under the mat. How many disasters in world and Church history might have been averted if only action had been taken in time! Churchill maintained that there could hardly ever have been a war more easy to prevent than World War II, if only the right preventive action had been taken in time. He himself always kept on his desk a printed notice which read "Action This Day."

Strange things have been brought into courts of law—such things as weapons, letters, photographs and articles of clothing. They are called "exhibits" and are used as evidence of the innocence or guilt of some accused person. But probably the strangest object ever to be produced in a court was a bowl of water. It was not an exhibit, but an excuse, a pretext for a great travesty of justice. It was the bowl of water in which Pilate washed his hands at the trial of Jesus.

Pilate knew that Christ was innocent and he seemed anxious to free Him, but instead, he did nothing. Literally, he washed his hands of the troublesome affair. Why? The cost was too great. Pilate had come to know our Lord a little and he admired and liked what he had learned, but he had been warned, "If you free this man you are no 'Friend of Caesar'" (Jn. 19:12). Afraid of losing favor, he did nothing.

There are many people in the world exactly like Pilate. There are those who have come to know Christ a little and admire Him but have done nothing about it. "Of course I am nothing," they say, "but if I had a religion, I would be a Catholic." Then there are the Catholics who say, "I don't go to church, but I don't do anyone any harm." And there are those who avoid all involvement.

Early in 1973, a teenage Mexican boy in California was given an award for rescuing three children from a burning automobile while twenty people looked on and did nothing.

We all tend to overlook our sins of omission, to forget the things we have failed to do and to ignore those opportunities we have of doing good and of giving happiness. Apathy, selfishness and the unwillingness to pay a price make us all the counterpart of Pilate.

In our human experience it seems that nothing is really worth having unless a price has been paid for it in toil, struggle and suffering. Madame Curie's heroic efforts in the discovery of radium illustrated this principle. After years of patient research, she and her husband set to work to produce radium. Often cold and hungry, they worked in a miserable shed that had a leaky roof and a dirt floor. On a rickety old stove they boiled down and refined eight tons of ore, and after four years of this drudgery, they finally produced one decigram of precious radium—about the size of a small pea.

"Labor conquers all things," said Virgil, the Roman poet. Horace, another writer of antiquity, wrote, "Life gives nothing to man without labor." As an axiom observes, "Nothing comes from nothing."

When God called Moses to deliver Israel from the Egyptians, Moses was appalled. Who was he to face the military might of Egypt? He was not even eloquent.... But God brushed aside his excuses. "What is that in your hand?" "A staff" (Ex. 4:2). It was something, and it was enough. "Take this staff in your hand; with it you are to perform the signs" (Ex. 4:17).

"How many loaves have you?" (Mk. 6:38) Christ asked His apostles. He wanted their cooperation. "Fill these jars with water" (Jn. 2:7), He bids the servants at the wedding feast at Cana. When He heals the sick, He requires them to cooperate with Him by their belief and trust. In the parable of the talents, He praises those who put their God-given ability to work, but He condemns the man who buried even only one talent.

We must, then, work out our salvation. "God who created us without our aid," says St. Augustine, "will not save us except with our aid." "We must pray as if everything depended on God," declares St. Ignatius, "and act as if everything depended on our own efforts."

We may feel helpless when we consider the vastness of world problems. We wonder what we can possibly do about any of them. God says to each of us, "What have you got?" If there is anything in ourselves or in our surroundings that we can improve, let us do it. A small step forward is better than standing still. It is better to try and fail than just to complain and do nothing.

It was said of Christ that "He went about doing good works" (Acts 11:38), and people praised Him because they said, "He has done everything well" (Mk. 7:37). That little word "do" was often on His lips. "Whoever does the will of my heavenly Father is brother and sister and mother to me" (Mt. 12:50). "I have come to do the will of him who sent me" (Jn. 6:38). He scorns all pious lip-service. "None of those who cry out, 'Lord, Lord will enter the kingdom of God but only the one who does the will of my Father in heaven" (Mt. 7:21).

He makes it clear also that love of our neighbor is something more than benevolent feelings. He ends His great story of the compassionate Samaritan with the words, "Go and do the same" (Lk. 10:37). He reminds us of all the things we want from others—forgiveness when we have done wrong, help when we are in need, kindness when we have been hurt, comfort when we are in distress, and encouragement when we are lonely and dispirited. Very well, but others, too, have those needs, so we must always keep in mind Christ's words, "Treat others the way you would have them treat you" (Mt. 7:12).

Lastly, we should never forget the Lord's great precept regarding the Eucharist. "Do this as a remembrance of me" (Lk. 22:19). The Mass, Holy Communion and prayer in general are the highest and noblest forms of activity possible to us. Without this spiritual activity, no lasting good can be achieved.

"Unless the Lord build the house,
they labor in vain who build it" (Ps. 127:1).

Mother Theresa of Calcutta is world-famous for her tireless and selfless work for the sick and the destitute. In an interview, she said that the Mass is the spiritual food that sustains her, without which she could not get through one single day or hour of the dedicated life she has chosen.

This life of ours is given us for a purpose. It is meant to be a time of preparing, planting and sowing, of toiling, building and doing. We are called to be co-workers with Christ in our salvation and sanctification, and in that of the world. "Whatever you do," exhorts St. Paul, "whether in speech or in action, do it in the name of the Lord Jesus. Give thanks to God the Father through him" (Col. 3:17).

When our time of judgment comes, we can be certain there will be no miscarriage of justice as there was at our Lord's trial. Our judgment will be merciful, but it will be searching. "Whoever acts unjustly will be repaid for the wrong he has done. No favoritism will be shown," writes St. Paul (Col.

3:25). God will render to everyone according to his or her works—and omissions. "I was hungry and you gave me no food, I was thirsty and you gave me no drink. I was away from home and you gave me no welcome, naked and you gave me no clothing. I was ill and in prison and you did not come to comfort me" (Mt. 26:42-43). We dare not go before Him empty-handed.

Communication with God

A story is told of a young lady in wartime receiving a letter from her soldier sweetheart, but inside the envelope there was nothing except a small piece of paper from a censor. On it was the terse message, "Your boy friend still loves you, but he talks too much."

Much fun is made of love letters, those wildly written expressions of love with their repetitions and exaggerations, their use of poetry and their clumsy attempts to describe deep emotions. Yet love letters are very human documents and they can be very precious to their recipients. It is said that the wife of Tolstoy, the great Russian novelist, used to beg her husband, in her old age and just before their tragic parting, to read to her the love letters he had written her when he was a young man.

Most people find any kind of letter-writing irksome and difficult, and probably few of us are good letter-writers. We usually have plenty to say, but our problem is how to put thoughts and feelings into words. So often our letters are affected and uninteresting.

The apostles experienced something of the same difficulty in their communication with God. They told our Lord about their problem, "Lord, teach us to pray" (Lk. 11:1). They did not ask to be taught some prayers—they were already familiar with the beautiful prayers composed by David and the prophets. Their problem concerned the manner and method of praying. And so Christ does not say, "This is the prayer you must always use," but, "When you pray, say..." (Lk. 11:2). The Lord's Prayer is a pattern or example of prayer, and we shall pray better if we model our prayers on it.

Simplicity is its great characteristic. It does not begin with an elaborate form of address. It is a series of remarks such as a child might make to his father. It is so simple that a child can understand it, but so profound that we never exhaust its meaning.

Prayer should be natural and suited to our individual personality. If by temperament I am emotional or matter-of-fact, my prayers should be the same. I am insincere if, for instance, I ask God to take me to Himself when I don't really want this, or if I say I am the greatest sinner when I really don't think so. We can no more fit ourselves into someone else's prayers than we can into their clothes or shoes.

We do not pose and make speeches to our close friends; our conversation is open and unaffected. So should our prayer be. "The Lord used to speak to Moses face to face, as one man speaks to another" (Ex. 33:11). Doubtless Moses replied with equal openness and affection.

This does not mean that we should never use prayerbooks or set forms of prayer. These can often help us to express in appropriate words our inward thoughts and feelings, and they can assist us when we are tired or distracted.

It is precisely because prayer is communication and conversation with God that we find it difficult to pray. Prayer is defined as the raising of the mind to God—the upraised hands are a symbolic gesture expressing this elevation. Now it is obviously easier to control the body than the mind, and further, it is easier to think of visible, tangible things than it is to think about the invisible and incomprehensible God.

Perhaps sometimes we begin our prayers with the best of intentions, we start straight away making requests, and then we find we have no more to say. We began in the middle, instead of starting with some truth, or some little piece of knowledge about God. The liturgical prayers of the Church begin with some brief assertion: "Almighty Father, by the self-abasement of your Son, you raised a fallen world. Grant...."

Unless we first think of some truth concerning God, our prayers are apt to be dull and lifeless. When we get to know our friends more intimately and experience their kindness and goodness, we are drawn closer to them. Better knowledge of God will increase our faith and trust in Him and it will enrich our prayers.

But the essential benefit of having an increased knowledge of God is that we want to praise Him more joyfully and wholeheartedly. Herein lies the deepest joy and satisfaction of prayer. We are lifted up out of ourselves and we find fulfillment of that deeply-rooted instinct of our nature to worship and adore.

The saints experienced this intense delight to the full; they became quite oblivious of their surroundings, and often heavenly mysteries and secrets were revealed to them in these moments of ecstacy. The majority of us have only known such happiness faintly and momentarily, nor must we selfishly seek it. The saints also experienced corresponding dryness in prayer.

The Lord's Prayer shows us that God wants us to praise Him. A scholarly but eccentric man said he had crossed out in his Bible all the words praising God because he explained, "God is a gentleman and He would find such adulation distasteful." Sincere praise, however, is not flattery. It is an expression of gratitude. We must, as God's creatures, give Him due acknowledgement and glad submission.

For almost all of us, distractions in prayer are inevitable, and perhaps we shall be less discouraged if we recognize this fact. We can even turn them into prayer. Weariness, worry, doubt and fears are what frequently distract us, and if we patiently accept them, lay them in spirit before God, confide in Him about them and beg His help and guidance, we shall eventually turn them to good account.

The number of books written about prayer must be beyond counting, but the Our Father contains all we really need to know. Probably the best advice ever given on prayer is that we learn to pray by praying, and to pray well by praying often. To be able to have such a close personal relationship with God may not be easy—even human relationships are not always easy to maintain—but for the creature to have the power to speak to the Creator is an immense and glorious privilege. It can only be to our own shame and loss if we do not use it.

Of what better worth are men than dumb beasts
If knowing God, they raise not their hands in
prayer?

Lonely Hands Outstretched

Perhaps one of the strangest remarks on record is that made to a journalist by John Grundy, the twenty-six-year-old athlete competing in a marathon walk. "Come and join me," he begged. "Loneliness is the worst thing about this race; I can stand almost anything but that."

Loneliness should not be confused with solitude. Sometimes solitude can be both necessary and enjoyable. There are times when we feel we must be alone, either to solve some problem or just to quiet frayed nerves. Even in grief we sometimes say, "Please, just leave me alone." The Gospel tells us that Christ Himself needed solitude for recollection and prayer: "...remaining there alone as evening drew on" (Mt. 14:24).

But loneliness is different. It is a very great suffering. The Bible tells us, "It is not good for the man to be alone" (Gn. 2:18), and it warns us, "Woe to the solitary man! For if he should fall, he has no one to lift him up" (Eccl. 4:10). Loneliness is that desolate feeling of being useless and helpless, the bitter feeling of being unloved and unwanted.

Mother Theresa of Calcutta told an interviewer: "In these twenty years of work among the people, I have come more and more to realize that it is being unwanted that is the worst disease any human being can ever experience. Nowadays we have found medicine for leprosy and lepers can be cured. For all kinds of diseases there are medicine and cures. But as for being unwanted, unless there are willing hands to serve and there's a loving heart to love, I don't think this terrible disease can ever be cured."

We are all lonely in the sense that we all experience varying degrees of loneliness at different times—a child going to a new school, people moving into a strange neighborhood, a person who has a long illness, the disabled and the bereaved. Not even the most gregarious can always escape the misery of loneliness. Our Lord Himself experienced loneliness; He would not have been truly human and a sharer in our sufferings had He shielded Himself from so universal a pain. Especially in the closing hours of His earthly life, in the garden of Gethsemani and on Calvary, He endured a loneliness and an abandonment beyond all human understanding.

It has been well said that no man is an island. In each of us there is a need for love and companionship. We strive all our lives to break through the barrier of loneliness and make some contact with another searching soul and with the One whom all seek—God Himself.

We hear many complaints of loneliness today, and this may seem strange because our greatly improved modern communications should have removed many of the old barriers between people. However it is said that on the average, people are living twenty years longer than they did. There are more elderly people living now, and it is most of all in the evening of life that we are alone and may become lonely. Byron wrote long ago,

"What is the worst of the woes that wait on age?
To view each loved one blotted from life's page,
And be alone, as I am now."

If they are in reasonably good health, some old people live happily alone, having wisely surrounded themselves with many interests. Rather than dread old age, it will be better for us if we can look upon a long life as a blessing.

"To have entered and now to have completed my eightieth year does not cause me any anxiety," Pope John observed. "In fact, it helps to keep me serene and confident. As always, I desire nothing more or less than what the Lord continues to give. I thank and bless Him every day and I am ready for anything."

But some older people need help. They are ailing or cannot easily get about. They feel they are a hindrance and a burden. Their closest relatives and friends have died. "We die alone," said Pascal. Perhaps God permits us to suffer this pain of loneliness so that we may gradually draw closer to Him and better realize our helplessness and dependence on Him. And doubtless He gives patience and courage to many of the old and lonely. Often we can envy them, their deep faith and unruffled tranquillity, their remarkable ability to adapt to change and to grow old graciously and cheerfully.

Nevertheless, there are many old people who live alone and who are forgotten. They need our help. In assisting them, we might perhaps learn how to cope with old age when our own turn comes. Sometimes it is just enough to visit and encourage them. People living alone tend to be introspective and anxious. They are often more afraid of becoming incapacitated than they are of death itself. And don't we all have a special dread that when we grow old we shall become feeble-minded and senile?

The recent pronouncements of medical research should allay our fears. Doctors now declare that senility is avoidable even without the use of drugs, and it can often be cured. The remedy is very simple and consists in keeping the mind active and in shape. We need mental as well as physical gymnastics, because the brain, like any other part of the body, becomes "flabby" when not exercised. *We rust out quicker than we wear out.*

Old people should be encouraged to be active and interested, to learn a new skill—perhaps even a new language; to keep themselves smart; to avoid stress, worry and self-pity; and if possible, even to help others. As we get older we are inclined to live in the past, but Fred Astaire, still dancing in his seventies, attributes his remarkable agility to living always in the present.

A Maryland senior citizen, at eighty-five, gets up at five-thirty every morning and reads current literature for several hours. Moses, Segovia, Michelangelo, Pope Leo XIII, Toscanini and Churchill are only a few among the great ones in history who were active right to the end of a ripe old age.

There must be many little ways in which we can help to ease the pain of loneliness. It is something to have the shelter of a roof and four walls, but sometimes these can come to have the isolation of a prison. It means a lot to elderly people when they are taken for an outing in a car to the country, or to church, or to do some shopping, or to visit friends.

People who live alone are always cheered by a friendly letter, too. A newspaper has the latest world news, but what is this in comparison with the interest of receiving a personal message? A little gift of flowers or something home-cooked shows our interest and concern. Just to stop by and encourage people to talk, or to ask for some information or advice lets them know they are respected and wanted.

An apostolate to the elderly and the lonely may not be spectacular, but it is a work of tender mercy, and it is doing to others what you hope may one day be done to you.

By nature St. Peter seems to have been fiercely independent, and Christ made him supreme head of the Church, but there is deep pathos and meaning in the last recorded words our Lord spoke to him,

"I tell you solemnly:
as a young man
you fastened your belt
and went about as you pleased;
but when you are older
you will stretch out your hands..." (Jn. 21:18).

Friendship

A war story described a night patrol penetrating into enemy-occupied territory. It was ambushed and had to withdraw hurriedly. One man, believed to have been killed, was left behind. A friend of the missing soldier begged to be allowed to go back to make sure. Reluctantly, the commanding officer gave permission. A few hours later the soldier returned alone, and the officer said to him, "I knew it was no use. I should not have let you take the risk."

"But, sir, it was worth the risk," the young soldier replied. "He was still alive when I found him, and he smiled and said, 'I knew you would come.' I did what I could for him before he died."

There are many stories told about friendship. Centuries ago, the pagan Cicero wrote a book about it, yet it hardly needs description or explanation. Friendship is not something mysterious and exotic, nor is it just a warm feeling of attraction. Real friendship is the strong attachment of affection and esteem between people; it is something permanent and implies loyalty, sacrifice, and the desire to please and to help.

"I haven't a friend left in the world," is the sad remark one often hears nowadays. Is friendship dying out? Simon Strimsky said, "New York has more hermits than will be found in all the forests, mountains and deserts of the United States." Modern life tends to be more and more impersonal. People are shut away in huge blocks of apartments. The daily rush and whirl, and such things as television, seem to work against "togetherness," and make us self-centered. So it is that there are perhaps more people now who are lonely and friendless. They are to be pitied.

"Life without a friend," says an old adage, "is death without a witness."

Shakespeare seemed uncertain and even cynical about friendship: "Most friendship is feigning, most loving mere folly." With its customary profound knowledge of psychology and human nature, the Bible gives a warning:

"Let your acquaintances be many,
but one in a thousand your confidant.
When you gain a friend, first test him,
and be not too ready to trust him.
For one sort of friend is a friend when it suits him,
but he will not be with you in time of distress.
Another is a friend who becomes an enemy,
and tells of the quarrel to your shame....
When things go well, he is your other self,
and lords it over your servants;
But if you are brought low, he turns against you
and avoids meeting you.
Keep away from your enemies;
be on your guard with your friends.
A faithful friend is a sturdy shelter;
he who finds one finds a treasure.
A faithful friend is beyond price,
...a life-saving remedy..." (Sir. 6:6-9, 11-16).

Every country has its praise of friendship: "We can live without brothers but not without friends."

"When a friend asks, there is no tomorrow."

"A friend may well be reckoned the masterpiece of creation."

"A faithful friend is the medicine of life." Even the ascetical Thomas à Kempis, in his *Imitation of Christ,* makes the observation, "Without a friend you cannot live well"; but he goes on to say, "And if Jesus be not your friend above all other friends, you shall indeed be sad and desolate." It is immensely consoling to us if we are certain that such a relationship really exists between God and us. Do we look upon God as our very dear friend, in much the same way as we have come to regard certain people?

The Bible describes Abraham as "the friend of God" and tells of God speaking to Moses as "one man speaks to another" (Ex. 33:11). The Israelites of ancient times were deeply conscious of the fact that they had been singled out from all other nations, and a friendship pact had been made by God with them. There are scriptural types and examples of a divine friendship. Such is the friendship between David and Jonathan: "Jonathan had become as fond of David as if his life depended on him; he loved him as he loved himself" (1 Sm. 18:1), and that between Ruth and Naomi: "Wherever you go I will go,...your people shall be my people, and your God my God" (Ru. 1:16).

Christ came as a friend. He could have come in many other ways, but He chose this way and this is how He is best remembered. Perhaps there is a danger here of sentimentalizing our Lord, but the plain truth is that He once came seeking and still seeks human friendship. He was under no illusions. There is nothing sentimental about His words on true friendship:

"There is no greater love than this:
to lay down one's life for one's friends" (Jn. 15:13).

He does not romanticize friendship, for He knew that He had come to His own and His own did not receive Him; it had been foretold of Him that He would be wounded in the house of His friends! (cf. Zec. 13:6). He understood only too well that "most friendship is feigning, most loving mere folly," that one of His apostles would betray Him, another would deny Him, and His own people would hand Him over to a foreign power.

Yet He deliberately chose human friendship.
"You are my friends
if you do what I command you.
I no longer speak of you as slaves....
Instead, I call you friends....
It was not you who chose me,
it was I who chose you..." (Jn. 15:14, 15, 16).

There were some who were privileged to be His special friends—the apostles, Lazarus and his two sisters, and doubtless many others, but there is never any indication that His friendship with them was exclusive. He is the friend of publicans and of social outcasts such as lepers, of those who are not of His race—the despised Samaritan and the detested Roman—of little children and of sinners. He was the friend of all who wished to have His friendship.

We appear in various guises to different people. To the politician, you are a voter; to the doctor, a patient; to the storekeeper, a customer; and to the world, just one of its many inhabitants. But to our Lord, the Christian is always a friend. He has given us every proof of the reality of this relationship.

Each of us can use St. Paul's words, "...[He] loved me and gave himself for me" (Gal. 2:20). And St. John wrote,

"The way we came to understand love
was that he laid down his life for us..." (1 Jn. 3:16).

What does Christ's friendship mean to us? As with every friendship, it means companionship. Francis Bacon said, "A crowd is not company," but it is even said that, "Two is company, three is a crowd." Although our Lord is the friend of millions, yet because of His divinity, we can look upon Him as belonging exclusively to each one of us.

His friendship means we possess a peace such as the world can neither give nor take away, peace of mind and conscience, the peace of knowing that between us and Him there are no obstacles. Such barriers should never exist between friends.

His friendship means we have the sympathy and help only a friend can give. Cervantes said, "In all misfortunes the greatest consolation is a sympathetic friend." Christ is truly compassionate. A person who is compassionate identifies himself with another's sufferings; he literally suffers with the other. The Incarnation is God's complete identification with human joys and sorrows. Christ participated in the joyous wedding celebration of Cana, and He wept at the grave-side of His friend, Lazarus.

His friendship means our relationships with others will become better. We shall respect others, especially the unfortunate and the needy, because they are His friends. It has been pointed out that the New Testament records forty people as having been healed by Christ. Of this number, thirty-four were either brought to Jesus or He was taken to them—by friends. Only six poor souls found their way unaided to Christ. "I assure you, as often as you did it for one of my least brothers, you did it for me" (Mt. 25:40).

His friendship means we shall find it easier to pray. Our attitude towards Him will be one of complete trust. Like any friend, He will be interested in everything that concerns us, and sometimes our prayers will be similar to the happy and intimate conversation between friends. His interests will also be ours. A one-sided conversation is selfish and boring.

Finally, Christ's friendship means the security we all need and cannot find in a world that is constantly changing. Human beings can be very fickle and unpredictable. Friendships often fade out. Perhaps our habits and interests change, and we outgrow a friendship, or it may be that distance and other things intervene, and our friendship dies. Long ago, Plutarch sorrowfully observed, "A constant friend is a thing hard to find." But the psalmist praises God because He is unchanging.

"Of old you established the earth,
and the heavens are the work of your hands.
They shall perish, but you remain
though all of them grow old like a garment.
Like clothing you change them, and they are changed,
but you are the same, and your years have no end" (Ps. 102:26-28).

Christ is our "sure shelter," our unchanging friend. "Who will separate us from the love of Christ?" asks St. Paul. "Trial, or distress, or persecution, or hunger, or nakedness, or danger, or the sword? ...For I am certain that neither death nor life, neither angels nor principalities, neither the present nor the future, nor powers, neither height nor depth, nor any other creature, will be able to separate us from the love of God that comes to us in Christ Jesus, our Lord" (Rom. 8:35, 38-39).

What does our friendship mean to Christ? On the face of it, little but disappointment and loss. Christ has the fullness of the Godhead and nothing can be added to Him. He does not need us or our friendship. But although He may not need us, *He wants us.* The act of creation gave joy to God. "Goodness is diffusive of itself."

"Friends share all things in common," said Diogenes. Christ wants our friendship. Nothing but the best is worthy of Him, so we must be prepared to give Him a loyal friendship, even if it costs all we have to give. Such a friendship can be what Scripture itself describes as "a life-saving remedy" (Sir. 6:16).

Disciplined Disciples

The American artist Benjamin West declared that it was his mother's kiss that made him an artist. As a child, he sat one day on the floor in his home with paper scattered untidily around him and paint all over his clothes. He was afraid of what his mother would say about the mess, but when she entered the room, instead of angrily scolding him, she kissed him and said, "Some day you will be a great artist."

Unfortunately, there are probably more stories told of the harm done by anger than of the good effects of mildness.

Kaiser Whilhelm had a deformed arm, and it is said that this irritated his mother so much she came to hate him and would sometimes say to him, "Get out of my sight, you cripple!" This treatment from his own mother warped his personality; he developed an inferiority complex and became aloof and arrogant.

One mother's sympathetic understanding produced a world-famous artist, while another's cruel anger perhaps helped to cause the holocaust of a world war. It is a sobering thought. Someone has said, "Anger is like a strong medicine, which if it is used in the right way, can do infinite good but which, if it is used in the wrong way, can do infinite harm."

"But is not anger something essentially evil?" some may ask. Even the pagan writer Horace said, "Wrath is a transient madness." An angry person seems to have lost all control. Franklin said, "A man in a passion rides a mad horse." The Bible praises meekness:

"A mild answer calms wrath,
but a harsh word stirs up anger" (Prv. 15:1).

Our Lord taught that there is a joy and blessedness in meekness: "Blest are the lowly; they shall inherit the land" (Mt. 5:5).

Whenever we hear anyone described as meek, we probably form an unfavorable mental picture of someone who is timid and subservient, weak and too cowardly to stand up for himself. Words, like human beings, often change and deteriorate, and in the New Testament, the Greek word for meekness (which is a translation of the Aramaic word used by Christ) has a more agreeable meaning.

The word "meekness" is the word the Greeks used when describing a horse that had been broken in and was harnessed. Instead of running about wild, it was trained and gave useful service. The same word was also used of a strong man who exercised his power not as a tyrant, but with kindness and gentleness.

The Latin word for mild, *mitis,* has a similar pleasant meaning, for it was used of a mature, mellowed and well-adjusted person, one who is disciplined and experienced, who is not easily provoked to unreasonable anger, and who is not quick to take offense. The mild person is stable and tranquil, neither slack and over-permissive nor quick-tempered and quarrelsome.

Anger is far from being an evil thing in itself. It is a strong emotion usually aroused by some insult or injury, or even by the fear of injury. Used properly, it has helped to abolish many injustices, such as cruelty, slavery and poverty. St. Paul said, "If you are angry, let it be without sin" (Eph. 4:26). What are the rules for anger?

To be justified, anger must be anger for a proper reason. Sometimes we are angry just because we are in a bad mood or because life is difficult. When things go wrong, our immediate reaction is to find a scapegoat; anyone will do, so long as we can blame them rather than ourselves.

Anger should always be kept under control. An uncontrolled outburst of temper shows the immaturity of the spoiled child.

At a United Nations meeting, the Russian Premier Kruschev banged on the table with his shoe. Macmillan, the British Prime Minister, raised a laugh when he turned to an interpreter and said with imperturbable calm, "I would like a translation of that."

Lastly, our anger must not be prolonged. "The sun must not go down on your wrath" (Eph. 4:26). We must not bear ill-will. Indeed, short-lived anger is often a sign that the anger was fully justified. It was completely selfless. When anger is for the sake of others, it is usually of the right kind. It is not meant to destroy, but to save and to perfect.

We sometimes see our Lord angry in the Gospels. He was angry with the Pharisees who tried to prevent His healing people on the Sabbath; He was angry with the tricksters in the Temple who robbed the poor; He was angry with the Scribes who made life unbearable by their concern over every little detail of the Law; and He was angry with Peter and the disciples whenever they adopted a worldly outlook or lacked faith in the Father.

But His anger was utterly unselfish. He was never angry at injuries inflicted on Himself. "When he was insulted, he returned no insult. When he was made to suffer, he did not counter with threats" (1 Pt. 2:23). During His unjust trial He kept silent. When Judas betrayed Him and Peter denied Him, no angry outburst escaped His lips. When He was mocked and spat upon, no word of reproach came from Him. And He faced the cruelty of His executioners with prayers for their forgiveness.

He wishes us, His disciples, to imitate Him. "Learn from me, for I am gentle and humble of heart" (Mt. 11:29). His meekness is the right kind of meekness, the meekness that spreads happiness, the meekness of a properly adjusted person. There is a joy that comes from a perfect submission to God and from a complete trust in Him so that we accept whatever happens to us as being for our ultimate good.

There is also a happiness in being mature and self-disciplined, because in our relationships with others we enjoy the peace and satisfaction that comes from being always tolerant, sympathetic and kind, patient and restrained. Instead of allowing ourselves to be selfishly angry, we generously expend our strength and energy for others, especially in the defense and support of the very young and the very old, the weak and the needy.

Angel of the World

A group of tourists was being shown around Beethoven's old home. In an upstairs room stood the composer's own piano. The guide explained that in this very room Beethoven had composed the "Moonlight Sonata." A young woman who was present sat down at the piano and began playing the sonata, but she stopped when she heard the guide saying that the great Paderewski had recently visited the house.

"And I'll bet he did just what I'm doing!" she exclaimed. "I'll bet he played the sonata. Boy, I wish I could have heard him!"

The guide shook his head. "No, madam. We asked him to do so, but he refused. He said he was not worthy."

Reverence means to regard someone or something with affectionate awe and respect. It has been described as one of the flowers of Christian civilization, and Shakespeare called it "angel of the world." In our present age, reverence has lost its bloom, and fools walk boldly where angels once feared to tread. The outward expressions of reverence, such as solemn divine worship and ceremonial, respect for God's laws and for the sacredness of human life, and even such commonplaces as courtesy and decent behavior tend to be regarded by some as irrelevant and insincere.

Reverence is essential for religion. A writer has said, "Reverence is the secret of religion and happiness. Without reverence there is no faith nor hope nor love. Reverence is the motive of each of the commandments of Sinai—reverence of God, of our neighbor, of ourselves. Humility is founded on it, piety is conserved by it, purity finds in it its buckler and shield...Satan is Satan because he is irreverent."

The reason why reverence and religion are so closely interwoven is simply because God is God and we are His creatures. Belief in God is the basis of reverence. The Gospels speak again and again of the people being filled with awe and respect when they witnessed Christ's miracles. At the miraculous catch of fish, Peter fell on his knees before our Lord and said, "Leave me, Lord. I am a sinful man" (Lk. 5:8). Christ praised the faith of a pagan Roman soldier who had declared, "Sir,...I am not worthy to have you under my roof" (Mt. 8:8).

But can we be sure that God exists? Has today's advanced scientific thinking made belief in the existence of God impossible? Nowadays many think that solid reasoning is all against belief in God, and that religion is based solely on fear, ignorance and emotionalism. The sagacious Dr. Samuel Johnson once remarked, "People need more often to be reminded than instructed." The old familiar arguments for the existence of God may no longer be popular, but they have not been disproven, and it is good for us to refresh our memories.

First, look around you. There are men and women everywhere who still believe in God, and scientists and great thinkers are among them. You cannot prove God by putting Him in a test tube or a computer, but unbelief is unnatural and illogical.

The human mind is always asking "why" and "how," and it does not rest until it can understand something of the nature and purpose of things. Why does the universe exist, and how did it get here? Did it start with a big bang, or through some slowly evolving process? The scientists are puzzled and make guesses.

Common sense alone tells us that the universe could not have just arrived of its own accord. It could not have made itself any more than a heap of stones, timber and glass could become a great cathedral without a brain, a plan and a purpose. If the universe could not possibly have come into existence of itself, then there must have been some Being of intelligence who produced it and who had a purpose for it. Without an eternal, self-existing God, the universe does not make sense.

Next, look inside yourself. We can see signs of God's existence within ourselves. We do not need to be anthropologists or biologists to know the difference between human beings and animals. In our human nature we can see the things that make us transcend the animals—our ability to think and to plan, our power of speech, and our artistic appreciation and achievement. But it is our moral and spiritual awareness that makes the real cleavage between us and animals. We all have the certain knowledge of the difference between right and wrong, kindness and cruelty, truth and lies.

People may talk as much as they like about evolution; there always remains that inexplicable gap between the human and the animal world. Man is still part animal and sometimes behaves little better than one, but the similarities are as nothing compared with the differences. Where could man's mysterious mind have come from, except from some greater Mind? In our human experience, there is absolutely nothing that comes from just nothing. The biblical explanation cannot be improved upon. It describes God as saying, "Let us make man in our own image, after our likeness" (Gn. 1:26).

Finally, look at our Lord. In Him we have a proof, an argument, from history itself. Christ has been well described as the One who broke history in two. We date the history of the world before and after His coming. Every time we write the date on a letter, we remember that modern history is dated from the birth of Jesus in Bethlehem. It is a recognition of His unique place in the history of the world.

The stories about Christ could not have been imagined; the teachings of Christ could not have been invented; the worldwide and enduring influence of Christ cannot be explained unless He really lived and His story and the claims He made are true.

He made claims that could be made only by God Himself. He claimed divine origin,

"I solemnly declare it:
before Abraham came to be, I AM" (Jn. 8:58).

He claimed equality with God, "The Son of Man is lord even of the sabbath..." (Mk. 2:28). "The Father and I are one" (Jn. 10:30). He claimed that He had divine power and authority, "the Son of Man has authority on earth to forgive sins" (Mt. 9:6).

"Whatever I say
is spoken just as he [the Father] instructed me" (Jn. 12:50).

> "Whoever has seen me, has seen the Father" (Jn. 14:9).

As we look at Christ we are not only convinced that God exists, but we learn many things about God. We learn that God is holy and calls men and women to purity and holiness of life; that He is not remote and aloof, but loves each one of us; that He patiently seeks those who have turned from Him, and gladly forgives those who repent of their sins. And we learn reverence from our Lord—reverence for God, for others and for ourselves; reverence, and not fear.

Christ always showed a deep, affectionate respect for His Father. His chief concern was to please Him and carry out His will. He showed exquisite courtesy to Mary and Joseph, humbly submitting to them, serving and obeying them. He was considerate with His apostles, not compelling, but merely inviting them to follow Him; He was never anything but kind to His disciples.

If He had any favorites among the people, it was the outcast or the destitute. He was never harsh or overbearing in His attitude towards repentant sinners. Although He was harassed by throngs of people, He had time for everyone, even little children. He condemned all irreverence.

> "You shall do homage to the Lord your God; him alone shall you adore" (Mt. 4:10).
>
> "My house is meant for a house of prayer" (Lk. 19:46).

Reverence will enrich our lives. It will strengthen our links with God. Our prayers will be more fervent, and we shall serve Him more conscientiously. It will safeguard and ennoble our relationships with others. We shall be more tolerant and considerate, esteeming both young and old; the lowly and the influential; those who are agreeable and those who may be unlikable. It will teach us to have a proper respect for ourselves—for our minds and bodies.

The alcoholic, the drug addict and the sex-pervert are sad and shameful spectacles. If reverence were to disappear wholly from our world, it would be an even gloomier and more horrifying prospect, because it would mean that nothing would be sacred any longer. Mankind would be slipping rapidly down the slope to the jungle and barbarism.

The Extra Mile

The word "generous" has an interesting derivation. It comes from the Latin "genus" and "generosus." Originally, it meant "highly born," and later the word was applied to anyone who had a nobility of character, who was magnanimous and above anything petty or mean.

Generosity is a word that helps us to have a better understanding of God. We tend to have too small an idea of Him. Creation tells us about Him and it says that God is generous:

"The heavens declare the glory of God,
and the firmament proclaims his handiwork" (Ps. 19:2).

There is, for instance, the vastness of the universe. A simple illustration may help our imagination. We are told that if we think of the sun as a grapefruit, then a grain of sand forty feet away would be the earth, and another grain of sand a third of a mile away would be Pluto, the outermost planet of our solar system.

In his book, *The Mysterious Universe,* Sir James Jeans said: "The total number of stars in the universe is probably something like the total number of grains of sand on all the seashores of the world. The majority are so large that thousands of earths could be packed inside each and leave room to spare."

The conclusion is obvious. If the building is so immense, what must be the nature of the architect and builder? There can be nothing petty about Him! He is infinitely good and generous in all His ways.

But since this is true, what of famines and starving millions? It is indeed a great scandal that there should be gigantic food shortages, but how much of this is due to "man's inhumanity to man" and to human greed and neglect?

Early in this century, a scientist searched for a wheat that would ripen soon enough to escape the frosts of the Canadian fall. Eventually, he cultivated a single plant and fifteen years later, North American farmers harvested three hundred million bushels of wheat, every kernel of which was a descendant of the lone plant of 1903. Furthermore, it out-yielded its predecessors by 20%—enough extra wheat to provide a year's bread for fifteen million people. God is lavish and abundant in His giving, but man's ways are economics and stabilization of prices. Some farmers are being subsidized to limit their crops.

There were no limits to the generosity of Christ. The miracle at the wedding feast at Cana is an instance of this. Our Lord had not intended to show His divinity so early in His ministry, and it was not a matter of great importance, yet He was powerless to refuse His mother. He gave profusely—six water jars filled to the brim, each holding twenty to thirty gallons, which would total around five hundred bottles of the best quality wine!

Jesus showed the same generosity on the two occasions when He miraculously fed the people in the desert. Several baskets were filled with what was left after all had eaten as much as they wanted.

He was generous in His response to every need, generous in His kindness and forgiveness, generous with His care, concern and love.

Frequent reflection on God's generosity is a sure way to enrich our spiritual life. It will help us to pray better. Many of those inspired prayers, the psalms, are devoted entirely to praising God for His "generous kindness." Yet for so many of us, prayer means only petitions, and as a result, it is sterile.

The more convinced we are of the generosity of God, the stronger will be our trust in Him. Sometimes when people have to suffer some tragic loss or affliction, they protest, "What have I done to deserve this; why does God treat me like this?" In ancient pagan times, men and women believed that the gods were hostile and cruel.

Herodotus, a writer of antiquity, said that just as the tallest trees were the most likely to be struck by lightning, so any man who raised himself out of mediocrity was in danger of being struck down by the resentful gods. In all those pagan religions there was fear, but never love. It is important for us to build up a strong trust in the abundant goodness of God.

The fullest implication of God's generosity to us is shown in our Christian calling and character. As Christians, we are "nobly born." We are not just grains of sand or wheat; we are not just the created things of God; we are His children. We have been "re-created." We have been born again in Baptism and are sharers in the divine life, "heirs with Christ" (Rom. 8:17).

The nobility of our Christian birth should show itself in our behavior. "Be imitators of God as his dear children," says St. Paul (Eph. 5:1). There must be nothing petty, mean or spiteful in our thoughts and conduct. How warmheartedly we respond to any generosity that is shown us—to the friend who puts himself out for us, to the storekeeper who takes a little trouble to satisfy us. Should we not respond warmly to God's tremendous generosity?

We can begin in small ways. The "highly born" show their nobility of character especially in the little courtesies of everyday life. The "little bit extra" can make the difference between mediocrity and excellence.

In the British Museum there are *seventy-five* different versions of Gray's "Elegy"—the poet had rewritten the poem until he felt it was perfect! Elgar, the composer, took twelve years to write the music for Newman's "Dream of Gerontius." In a letter to his publisher, he said, "I don't want to send you the manuscript until I have been through it again and again, and after that, once more." We hardly serve God generously and as He deserves if we stop short at duties and commandments, and grudgingly do only the minimum required of us.

Christ once said, "Should anyone press you into service for one mile, go with him two miles" (Mt. 5:41). The extra prayer, Mass and visit to the Blessed Sacrament; the extra care to avoid complaints, gossip and unkind talk; the extra effort we put into our work; the extra consideration we give to others—all these are the extra miles that will show our generosity. And these little "extras" will prepare us for even greater acts of generosity.

Alaska was once described by a Pope as the hardest mission territory in the world. Several of the priests and brothers either froze to death, were drowned or died in plane crashes. They endured loneliness and hunger and many were broken in health.

The late Bishop O'Flanagan of Juneau once told of a missionary who worked in Alaska for forty years. He was very strong and sometimes would run ahead of the dogs beating trail, but on one occasion he went to the limits of endurance. He was on a long journey and he was cold and hungry. The guide was worn out and the dogs were tired. It became colder as night closed in upon the white wilderness. Finally, he became so exhausted and dispirited that he just sank down in the snow, and sobbed aloud that he could stand it no longer, that he was quitting, that he was through with everything.... It was a momentary spell of physical prostration and desolation. After it, he regained his courage and resumed his journey.

If we wish to be generous, we must be prepared to pay a price. We may not be called upon to have the heroic generosity of the saints and martyrs, but if our love of God is real, then we shall make generosity our constant aim.

"My dear Lord Jesus, teach me to be generous. Teach me to serve You as You deserve; to give and not to count the cost; to fight and not to heed the wounds; to toil and not to crave for rest; to labor and not to seek reward, except that of knowing that I am doing Your will."

Just for Today

Worry and fear are prominent characteristics of our age. In the United States, anxiety states are the commonest forms of mental illness, accounting for a tenth of a doctor's time and work. There is no doubt that modern life has added extra stresses and problems, but some of our fears are self-inflicted.

Christ taught a very simple remedy for worry and fear. "Today has troubles enough of its own" (Mt. 6:34). His meaning is clear: live each day as it comes; live in the present; live just for today. The remedy seems simple enough, but to carry it out requires some conviction and determination, because we tend to live either in the past or in the future, rather than in the present. To live exclusively in either past or future is unrealistic and can cause us undue worry and fear.

The past can be an illusion. We easily magnify the joys of the days that are gone. The "good old days" may not have been so good; we were younger then and small things appeared big, but if we were to go back to them, how small and shallow they would seem! We can always be grateful for happy memories without sighing our life away with regret. St. Augustine regretted his past, "Too late have I loved You..."

but he began life anew. We must prevent the past from reaching out its dead hand to paralize our efforts to reform, to find new friends, and other kinds of happiness.

The past can also poison the present. We can be haunted by the specters of past miseries and misdeeds. We can torture ourselves with remorse over the grief we caused others, or torment ourselves with regret for our mistakes or the good we neglected to do. The past is full of bitter accusations and we feel powerless, guilt-laden.

But we forget that past evils can be magnified. "When I was a child," wrote St. Paul (and perhaps he was thinking of when he persecuted the Church), "I used to talk like a child, think like a child.... When I became a man, I put childish ways aside" (1 Cor. 13:11). We may have done many wrongs in our earlier days, but perhaps we were immature then.

Repentance is the only way to conquer ghosts of the past, so that instead of being dreaded reminders, they become more like angels of good, making our hearts humble and contrite. A petition for forgiveness and a prayer for those we have wronged is the simplest and best remedy, if we cannot make up for the wrong by some concrete action. We can make amends by eradicating from our minds all grudges and resentment, and by practicing greater kindness to others in our present life. Archbishop Goodier wisely observed,

"Of all delusions, perhaps none is so great as the thought that our past has ruined our present; that the evils we have done, our mistakes and follies, have made all further hope impossible."

"Today has troubles enough of its own" (Mt. 6:34). When our Lord said this, He was referring to the harmful influence the future can have on us. "Enough, then, of worrying about tomorrow. Let tomorrow take care of itself" (Mt. 6:34). Jesus does not mean for us to ignore the future. But He is telling us to avoid over-anxiety about it. To be constantly preoccupied, worried and even fearful of the future is to lose all peace of mind and enjoyment of the present.

Experience shows that most of the things we worry about do not happen, and the worry itself is more distressing and harmful than the imagined evil.

A private tragedy was enacted recently in England. The newspapers reported briefly that an elderly retired army officer and his wife made a suicide pact. The husband thought he had cancer; they could not face the future; so they killed themselves. A post-mortem examination revealed no trace of the disease!

Worry is often a fear reaction over a future happening which may never materialize. Over-anxiety indicates a lack of trust in divine Providence. "Stop worrying, then.... Your heavenly Father knows all that you need. Enough, then, of worrying about tomorrow. Let tomorrow take care of itself. Today has troubles enough of its own" (Mt. 6:31, 32, 34).

Today, then, should always be our chief concern. Each day is a kind of lifetime in miniature. To awaken each morning is to be born again and to fall asleep at night is to die to the day. Of all the many kindnesses of God to man, is there any greater kindness than the arrangement He has made for us to live each day as a life apart, to make of each day a perfect thing, unspoiled by what may have been or by what might be? Yet we set this kindness aside so often.

One supreme advantage of living for just one day at a time is that we considerably lighten the burden of living. What we feel we cannot bear for a lifetime, we can endure for a daytime. We can guard our tongue and check our tempers; we can be unselfish and courageous, kind and considerate to others more easily for a day at a time. Robert Louis Stevenson wrote, "Anyone can live sweetly, patiently, lovingly and purely until the sun goes down."

"Finish every day and be done with it," advised Emerson. "You have done what you could; some blunders and absurdities have crept in; forget them as soon as you can. Tomorrow is a new day; you will begin it well and serenely, unencumbered by your old nonsense."

To live in the present, to be content in the present, to make the most of the present—this is our Lord's simple formula for happiness. St. Paul in his writings shows his impatience with his fellow Jews because they clung to the past and still had their expectations of a Messiah to come. "Now," he insisted, "Now is the acceptable time! Now is the day of salvation!" (2 Cor. 6:2) We, too, have the same fault. "Not now, but later on, I shall give more time to my soul, to prayer and to serving others; later, when I am freer and have more time...."

The French spiritual writer, Pere du Caussade, coined the expression "the sacrament of the present moment." The present, he explained, is like a life-giving sacrament. "What happens at each moment bears the imprint of the will of God.... How fitting then, to bless each moment, to treat it as something sacred, like a sacrament."

It is by living each day as it comes that we are able to show complete submission to God's will.

"Give us this day our daily bread," is our prayer. Like Cardinal Newman in his poem, "Lead Kindly Light," we leave the future and all it holds for us in God's hands.

"...the distant scene,
I do not ask to see; one step,
Enough for me."

It requires great faith and trust to be ready for and to live each day as it comes, but it is faith and trust that God wants from us—not regrets for the past nor fears of the future.

"Lord, for tomorrow and its needs
I do not pray;
Keep me, guide me, love me, Lord,
Just for today."

Acceptance

When, as a child, Christ was lost in Jerusalem, Mary His Mother asked, "Why have you done this to us?" (Lk. 2:48) Later, at Calvary, our Lord asked a similar question of His Father, "Why have you forsaken me?" (Mt. 27:46) Grief asked the question on each occasion.

At some time or other during life, the question is on the lips of every man and woman. "Why should this happen to me? What have I done that God should treat me like this?" And no answer seems to come that will ease the pain or lighten the burden. It helps little to be told in moments of grief that time will heal. It probably will, but meanwhile, the moments and days and even years of pain must be lived through. Nor does it hearten us to be reminded that there are others worse off, because this is merely reminding us that grief is widespread. As Tennyson wrote:

"That loss is common would not make
My own less bitter, rather more;
Too common! Never morning wore
To evening, but some heart did break."

We certainly cannot avoid life's pains and griefs, but can we make them bearable and even profit by them? Circumstances alone do not make us happy or unhappy. It is the way we react to them that determines our happiness. There are mainly two reactions to suffering; resentment or acceptance.

Resentment is a form of rebellion; one carries the burden of grief alone and makes it heavier. He becomes cynical and bitter about everything; he envies and hates others for the happiness they have; he leads a soured, unnatural existence. Resentment is not a healer but a killer. Certain bodily ailments are now called psychosomatic, for they are caused by sickness of the mind, such as fear, worry and resentment.

But resentment doesn't stop at poisoning mind and body; it destroys one's relationship with God. Belief in His existence goes, or He is seen as unjust and cruel. The resentful man rebels against Him. Christ said the kingdom of God is within man, but the kingdom of hell can be there, too.

The other reaction to pain and grief is acceptance. There is a fifteenth century cathedral that carries a cryptic inscription, "It is so. It cannot be otherwise." In life we meet many situations that cannot be otherwise: accidents and sickness; privations and disappointments; separations and bereavements; the consequences of our mistakes and sins. Often, we can do little else but say, "It is so. It cannot be otherwise." Or to use modern phrases, "Well, that's the way things are"; "it's just one of those things."

Psychologically, it is usually the best policy to accept inevitable situations, to adjust to them, to refuse to be overwhelmed by them, and as far as we can, to turn them to good account. The psychologist, William James, says, "Be willing to have it so. Acceptance of what has happened is the first step to overcome the consequences of any misfortune." Long ago it was said, "A good supply of resignation is of the first importance in providing for the journey of life."

The way of acceptance is not negative fatalism or escapism. It is squarely facing our grief and even profiting from it. It is not an easy way because it is the way of Christ, the saints and martyrs, and countless unknown heroes and heroines. But we are all stronger than we think. We have hidden resources of strength and courage waiting to be drawn upon.

The life of a great woman social worker illustrates this. She and her husband were on vacation in Europe. Their only child, a little girl, was eagerly awaiting their return. She had been put to bed the night they returned home, but at the sound of their arrival, she jumped out of bed, rushed to a banister rail, leaped on it to slide down, lost her balance, and fell.

"Never," said Mrs. Butler, "can I lose that memory—the fall, the sudden cry and then the silence. It was pitiful to see her helpless in her father's arms, her little drooping head resting on his shoulder, and her beautiful golder hair, all stained with blood, falling over her arm. Would to God I had died that death for her! If only we had been permitted one look, one moment of recognition."

How did she react to her grief? With resentment, self-pity or escapism? She rose up from it and devoted her life to caring for countless wayward and motherless girls. There was the perfect reaction of acceptance and turning loss into gain. Shakespeare wrote, "They say best men are moulded out of faults." Beethoven probably produced better music, and Tolstoy and Dante, better writings because of their tortured lives.

Very often it is those who have been reared in the hard school of toil and privation who are best equipped to meet life's trying situations. There are humorous stories as well as tales of tragedy told of the London wartime Blitz. One is about the old couple who were hurrying to an air-raid shelter. The wife wanted to go back to the house for her dentures, but her husband would not let her. "Come on, woman. It's not ham sandwiches they're dropping."

Then there was the little man standing in the street during a heavy raid. The noise of exploding bombs was deafening, but the man stood shaking his fist towards the sky and shouting angrily. His wife kept urging him to come indoors with the plea: "Come on inside and don't aggravate them!"

Christian acceptance means more than just, "It is so," and more even than the courageous, "Be willing to have it so." Our Lady said, "Let it be done to me as you say" (Lk. 1:38). Christ prayed, "Not my will, but yours be done" (Lk. 22:42). Our acceptance must be the willing submission to God's will. Perhaps we tend always to associate God's will with grief. We describe natural calamities as "acts of God" and carve on tombstones the sad words, "Thy will be done." But what is willed is intended, and above all else God intends us to have happiness, although His will is often obstructed. "If only you had known the path to peace this day; but you have completely lost it from view" (Lk. 19:42).

Only the acceptance of whatever God wills or permits can bring us true peace. Shall we not therefore begin now by patiently accepting the small everyday upsets, annoyances and frustrations, so that when heavier burdens are laid upon us, we shall have prepared ourselves to accept them?

Keeping Calm Thoughts

People in prominent positions are exposed to criticism and opposition. A story is told of a distinguished statesman who was being unfairly and continuously attacked by a conceited politician, but the statesman was always calm and unruffled. One day a friend asked him how he managed to keep his temper under such provocation.

"Well," replied the statesman, "perhaps it can best be explained by an incident from my childhood. We lived near a man whose dog, whenever there was a full moon, used to bark angrily, sometimes for an hour or so. It was very distressing for everyone except the owner of the dog, for he was deaf." Here the statesman paused while his friend waited expectantly.

"That's all there is to it," the statesman smiled. "The moon shone, the dog barked; the moon kept on shining, and after a while, the dog got tired of barking." The statesman kept on "shining" while waiting for his opponent to tire of "barking."

Patience is a lowly virtue, rather passive and negative – "the poor man's virtue," it has been called. Yet we all need it in our pressure-filled, hectic, present-day existence.

It may be a lowly virtue, but we should remember that God is patient. Patience is a characteristic of His work of creation. How old is the earth? Geologists speak of long ages of slow formation through periods of thousands of millions of years. "Geology is the study of God's patience." There is slow growth in nature: weeds may sprout quickly, but trees such as the enduring oak are slow-growing.

God is patient in His dealings with mankind. The Old Testament is a record of His patient endurance of human stupidity and wickedness. "The Lord...[is] slow to anger..." (Ex. 34:6) declared Moses. God delayed a hundred years before sending the deluge and He waited ten years before punishing Saul.

But most of all, it is the Gospels that reveal God's patience, for it is there we see that central figure, the calm and unhurried Christ. He was patient with the self-seeking, sensation-loving crowds; patient with His apostles and disciples, often so slow to believe and understand; patient with the hostile, as when He rebuked His disciples for wanting the destruction of a town that had refused them entry.

Jesus was especially patient in His sufferings. We readily make allowances for the impatience of those in pain, but no such allowances had to be made throughout the whole of Christ's sufferings. He remained silent during the hypocrisy of His trial. He was patient when His flesh was torn by the scourges, and He uttered no complaint when He was mocked and spat upon. Patiently He stumbled with the cross to Calvary and, nailed to it, He patiently endured every kind of torment until the end.

God's patience is inexhaustible: "...a merciful and gracious God...rich in kindness and fidelity, continuing his kindness for a thousand generations..." (Ex. 34:6-7).

Whether He is ignored, hated, denied, or outraged by His creatures, He waits patiently.

Christ told the story of the poisonous weed being sown by an enemy among the wheat. The farm-workers want to root it out at once, but the farmer counsels patience. "Let them grow together until harvest" (Mt. 13:30). Dangerous advice, that seems to overlook the contagious effects of evil! But God waits in order to bring good out of evil. He forgives more than He condemns. Yet although His mills grind slowly, they grind exceedingly small, so we must never abuse His patience.

We ourselves need to cultivate the virtue of patience. No great or lasting work was ever achieved without it. It is one of the ingredients of genius—the almost infinite capacity to keep trying. Since we live in an age that worships speed and quick results, patience is more necessary than ever, for it is difficult to avoid being caught up in the frenzied tempo, the inevitable stresses and pressures. We need more than a stoical patience. We need Christian patience, which will motivate us more effectively and turn to good account life's sufferings.

The word patience is derived from the Latin *patior*, "I suffer," and it is defined as the calm endurance of any pain or provocation. Theologically, it is that virtue which makes us accept with equanimity of soul all physical and spiritual sufferings for the love of God and in union with Christ. It is well to understand that patience involves suffering, but at the same time to remember:

"Patience is bitter, yet its fruit is sweet."

"How poor are they who do not have patience!" Shakespeare wisely observes: "What wound did ever heal but by degrees?"

Few of us are patient by nature. We need to acquire this valuable virtue. How can we set about it? First, we must introduce some periods of quiet reflection into our lives.

The novelist, Howard Spring, said that in the stressful months of 1940, he found it difficult to settle down to his work. One morning, he chanced to pick up and read a book of reflections of the Emperor Marcus Aurelius. It calmed and steadied his mind, and thereafter he formed the habit of beginning each day with a quiet reading—eventually from the Bible. He explained,

"It is so easy to begin the day with a rush through the morning mail, a rush through the morning paper, and a rush at the work in hand. It is like playing the fiddle before it is keyed up; it will be off-pitch all day."

Next, we need to reflect more on patience itself and the advantages it will bring us. Obviously those who are patient have a more pleasant, peaceful existence than those who are hasty, irritable and easily upset. Speaking to the apostles about suffering and persecution, Christ said, "By patient endurance you will save your lives" (Lk. 21:19). The patient person is self-possessed and well-balanced, sees things in their proper perspective, realizes we live in an imperfect world and that trials, pains and disappointments are unavoidable, but can be of value if they are patiently endured for the love of God in union with Christ. Says St. James, "See how the farmer awaits the precious yield of the soil. He looks forward to it patiently while the soil receives the winter and the spring rains. You, too, must be patient" (Jas. 5:7-8).

It will help if we begin each day with the resolution, "Whatever happens today, I shall keep my thoughts calm, cheerful and patient." A sense of humor is invaluable. Resolutely, we must avoid dwelling on our misfortunes, mistakes and failures. And we must rid ourselves of all resentment over injuries done to us and banish any desire to revenge ourselves. Instead, we must learn to check all external signs of impatience—the slammed door, the voice raised in anger, the hasty rejoinder.

If we have a true love of God and our neighbor, it will surely show itself in our practice of the lowly virtue of patience. "Love is patient; love is kind.... There is no limit to love's forbearance, to its trust, its hope, its power to endure" (1 Cor. 13:4, 7).

Our Lord Himself is our model and our greatest help in acquiring patience. "Learn from me, for I am gentle and humble of heart" (Mt. 11:29). In moments of pain, disappointment and irritation, the thought of Jesus will do more than anything else to encourage us to be patient. "When he was insulted, he returned no insult. When he was made to suffer, he did not counter with threats" (1 Pt. 2:23).

True Values

It was just after ten o'clock on the night of April 14, 1912, that the Titanic, the largest vessel then afloat, steamed into an iceberg in Mid-Atlantic, and four hours later went to the bottom. Much has been written of what took place in those four hours. Survivors spoke of the calm heroism of the Captain, the officers and the crew. They told of the band playing the hymn, "Nearer My God to Thee" and they said that many women who could have been rescued, refused the offer, preferring to drown with their husbands.

They told another story also, less courageous but more curious than any of these. A certain woman who had been allotted a place in one of the boats, asked if she might run back to her stateroom; she was given three minutes in which to do it. She hurried along the corridors already tilting at a dangerous angle, and crossed the saloon. Money and valuables littered the floor. Some people who snatched at their jewelry spilled it as they ran.

In her stateroom she saw her own valuables waiting to be picked up—she saw them but she ignored them. Instead, she picked up three oranges and raced back to her place in the boat.

That little incident is instructive. A few hours before, it would have seemed incredible to that woman that she could have preferred three oranges to all her valuables, but death had come to the Titanic, and in an instant all values were transformed. Precious things became worthless; worthless things became precious.

The Christian must always strive to regard objects and events from the viewpoint of eternity, to see them in a supernatural rather than a natural light. This is the only way in which to arrive at their true meaning and value.

Matthew and Luke narrate an incident that shows how in God's estimation a thing can have a totally different value from that set upon it by human beings. One day our Lord, probably tired, sat under a colonnade surrounding a court in the Temple of Jerusalem. He was watching the worshipers making their contributions. Among them were many who were very wealthy and who ostentatiously gave large sums. Then along came a poor widow; furtively she put in two little bronze coins. It was the minimal offering, for one coin would not have been enough.

What a trivial incident to be recorded for millions to read, while far more momentous things have been forgotten! But Christ was interested in this poor woman. No one else noticed her. The apostles were probably admiring and praising the large sums given by the rich people. They were judging by worldly standards. Our Lord saw it all differently.

"This poor widow has put in more than all the rest," Christ tells them (Lk. 21:3). The apostles must have been mystified. They had yet to learn that God's values are different from ours. So our Lord explained. "They make contributions out of their surplus, but she from her want has given what she could not afford—every penny she had to live on" (Lk. 21:4). Objectively her gift was almost worthless—

collection of such coins was more trouble than they were worth. But to her they meant her supper; she would have to go without her next meal or do some work to earn it.

We are not told whether Christ spoke to her, gave her a word of encouragement or offered her an alms. The poor woman did not even know she was being watched and praised by our Lord. But the objectively unimportant act had been lovingly noticed. Small and insignificant as it seemed, it derived its great spiritual value from the fact that it came from a heart filled with personal devotion, with deep faith, and most of all, it involved personal sacrifice. "She from her want has given what she could not afford—every penny she had to live on" (Lk. 21:4).

How consoling is this simple scene to us ordinary people, whose lives are filled with unspectacular routine! How well it reminds us that God's ways and values are different from ours! How it should encourage us to persevere, laying up treasure in heaven!

We might be tempted to think that God looks only on heroic deeds, lengthy prayers, great sacrifices. Our little commonplace lives, scrappy prayers and unimportant actions must pass unnoticed by Almighty God, we say. Then we think of the widow's mite. Heaven's arithmetic is different from ours. Nothing is too small or insignificant for Him who sees in secret and numbers the very hairs of our head. Every aspiration, every short prayer of faith, hope, love and gratitude; every resistance to sin and selfishness; every kindness to others counts with God. He values our desire to please Him, love Him and serve Him, especially when it involves real sacrifice.

Prophets Today?

Bishop Thomas Dunn of Nottingham, England, was a shrewd, saintly man who made several predictions which came true in his own lifetime. Occasionally, he ventured to forecast the more distant future. About the year 1930, he warned, "In fifty years' time there will be no more religion left in England except the Catholic religion—and there will be precious little of that."

His hearers were naturally incredulous because he spoke at a time when just the opposite was taking place. Vocations to the priesthood and the religious life were plentiful; there was an influx of converts; churches and schools were being built everywhere. A similar growth of Catholicism was taking place in many other countries. However, it is the usual fate of prophets to be scorned.

The prophets of the Old Testament days would seem to have had especially difficult and unenviable tasks. They were privileged to have been chosen by God and they were given a rare experience of Him; they were able to view the present and the future through the very "eyes of God." Nevertheless, they were sent to proclaim God's warning and demands. They had to be "signs" of the divine will in their own persons. Not only their words, but their whole lives had to speak of God. They were meant to be like beacon lights flashing warnings and encouragement in the darkness.

No one likes to be threatened. Because the prophets had to remind men and women of their duty to God and often to upbraid and correct them, they cannot have been popular. Christ speaks of the prophets being stoned and murdered.

Amos the prophet had an arduous assignment and he was unsuccessful. He was a sheep breeder and, therefore, not a poor man, but being a true son of the desert, he probably lacked the social graces. This must have put him at a disadvantage, since among other things, he had to condemn sophisticated city-life. His greatest difficulties, however, arose from the fact that he was sent to predict doom at a time when the Israelites were enjoying great prosperity.

He had three principal prophetic visions. In the first, he saw a swarm of devouring locusts devastating the land, and he interpreted this to mean famine for the people. In a second vision a great fire destroyed everything and this meant that homes and buildings were doomed. The third vision was the strangest of all and threatened the greatest catastrophe. It was of a bricklayer standing, plumb line in hand, against a wall full of ominous, widening cracks.

How alarmist and unreal these prophecies must have seemed to those who heard them! There was peace and security, the kingdom was visibly extending and growing in strength, new buildings were being set up. Almost everyone enjoyed great prosperity and plenty, and everywhere there was stability, wealth and progress.

Some thirty to forty years passed before the visions became reality. About the year 735 B.C., the Assyrians attacked, killing and plundering, sweeping through the land like a swarm of locusts. Town after town went up in flames. They harassed the Israelites for a considerable time and, finally, after a siege that lasted for three years, Samaria, the capital of Israel, fell. With it came the final collapse of the kingdom of the ten northern tribes, like some great wall disintegrating and crumbling into rubble.

Prosperity can be dangerous. The best of times can also be the worst of times. The possession of material things tends to make human beings selfish and greedy. Wealth can give a false sense of security and independence.

Behind the prosperity in this period of ancient Israel's history was neglect of God and widespread corruption and injustice. Although the people gave only a formal allegiance to God, He did not abandon them at once. He sent His prophet to warn and to recall them. He waited patiently, but when the years passed and they remained heedless, He was at last compelled to withdraw His protection and leave them to their self-appointed doom.

For many years now America and Europe have enjoyed a great measure of prosperity. While we can be thankful that there is less poverty and hardship for the majority of people, we need to be vigilant. People have become so involved in this life that many have forgotten there is any other. Irreligion and corruption have spread like a forest-fire, and ominous cracks are appearing in the walls of our civilization.

Prophets of doom are not lacking, and these are not the lone figures of earlier days, some of whom were fanatical in their words and behavior. Sober scientists, writers and politicians claim to have evidence of the approaching calamity. They are chiefly occupied with the environment and some of their statements are exaggerated, but there is some reason for their concern; sometimes they speak of even greater anxieties.

One shrewd observer has remarked that our society's earlier sense of moral order came from the Christian Faith, and now if people lose their sense of moral order, we will soon lose all other order—economic, political and social.

Is there anything we can do? We cannot claim to possess any prophetic powers, but within our very small sphere of influence, we can exercise one of the functions of a true prophet. The prophets were not restricted to uttering threats and forecasting doom. They were "signs" of God in their own persons. Not only their words, but their lives and behavior spoke of God. They were lights of hope and encouragement. Amos foretold a restoration and an even greater prosperity to come. His words must have heartened many a weary and despairing sufferer of injustice and poverty.

Each of us can be a tiny beacon of light shining out steadfastly in this twentieth century gloom and darkness. Christ said to His disciples, "You are the light of the world. ...your light must shine before men so that they may see goodness in your acts and give praise to your heavenly Father" (Mt. 5:14, 16). We need to show the light of our Christian Faith and hope, the light of our deeds of love, the light of our humble submission to God's will and the light of our courage and trust.

To Sir Harry Lauder, the Scottish singer of many years ago, no sight was more lovely in all bonny Scotland than the lamplighter coming down the darkened street. He said once in an address, "I love to part the curtains and peep out at the lamplighter, to trace his movements by the lamps he has lighted and the long trail of light he has left behind him."

Perhaps it may be that here and there some anxious and discouraged soul may be heartened to persevere or to try afresh in life because of the example we have given. If we cannot be prophets, at least we can be like the lamplighters of old and leave behind us a trail of light that will guide the steps of those who otherwise might have groped in darkness.

God's Guidance

A farmer hired a man to sort out his potato crop. The large, medium and small-sized were to be put in separate heaps. After a few days, the man came to the farmer in a worried state of mind. He complained of being exhausted and of having lost weight. In short, he wanted to quit. The surprised farmer asked if the work were too hard.

"No," the hired man replied, "but the decisions are killing me."

We cannot avoid having to make decisions and sometimes it can be a very worrying and wearying experience. Many of our decisions may not be important, but there are crucial occasions when we have to make a momentous decision that affects other people as well as ourselves. How we long for clear guidance! We ponder the problem and waver uncertainly between one choice and another. We seek advice, only to find that there are as many opinions as there are people. We pray, but often the mist does not lift, and we are left with the helpless feeling of being alone at crossroads without directions.

Animals do certain things instinctively, without ever having been taught. Birds build complicated nests and find their way unerringly over immense distances of land and sea. Yet for all our superior powers of reasoning, we often make the most ludicrous mistakes and afterwards reproach ourselves, "Why did I ever do such a stupid thing?"

Because doubt, uncertainty and indecision are so painful and distressing, we have urgent need of God's guidance in our affairs. Dare we think that almighty God actually concerns Himself about each of us and, in response to our earnest supplications, sometimes intervenes in our trivial affairs?

When astronomers tell us that the sun is only one of millions of stars, not even the biggest and brightest, and that the earth is so small in comparison with the rest of the universe, we realize our insignificance and ask as the psalmist did centuries ago, "O Lord,...what is man that you should be mindful of him...?" (Ps. 8:5)

However, mere size alone is not a reliable standard of value. A diamond could be more precious than a mountain, and men and women are more valuable than planets. "Astronomy may prove the insignificance of man, but man is still the astronomer."

Shakespeare said, "There's a divinity that shapes our ends, rough-hew them how we will." Most of us can look back on life and marvel at what seemed to be chance happenings—an unexpected meeting with someone, the missing of a train or an appointment, an accidental occurrence that altered our plans, some sudden inspiration or resolution that changed everything. Such things are too numerous and remarkable to be dismissed as accidents or coincidences. And moreover our prayers *are* answered.

As Christians, we cannot doubt God's loving care and guidance of every one of us. It is the recurrent theme of Christ's teaching. The Israelites, God's chosen people, believed God loved and protected their nation to the exclusion of the pagan and the wicked. But our Lord declared that God is a Father who makes the sun rise on the just and the unjust, who loves the prodigal as well as the good son and whose providence covers all creation, being extended even to the smallest and least important objects.

"Are not two sparrows sold for next to nothing [a penny]? Yet not a single sparrow falls to the ground without your Father's consent" (Mt. 10:29). This is one of Christ's sayings that is recorded by Matthew. Luke reports a slightly different one. "Are not five sparrows sold for a few pennies? Yet not one of them is neglected by God" (Lk. 12:6). The two different statements have a significant implication. A few pennies purchased not four but five sparrows. The extra one was thrown in; it had scarcely any value; it hardly counted at all. But our Lord is saying that it was not overlooked or forgotten by God. Indeed scholars tell us that the saying in the original Aramaic could mean that God sees the sparrow, not just when it falls lifeless to the ground, but every time it alights and hops on the ground.

Our Lord could not have been more explicit. The Father cares for each one of us. We are of greater value to Him than sparrows, or even stars. However little we may matter to others in this preoccupied and competitive world, we matter to Him. This is the basis for our belief that He guides us.

Since God does not force His guidance upon us, how can we obtain it so that the decisions we make may be prudent and wise? First, we must remember that it is part of God's Providence for us to use the mind He has given us. We cannot expect some sensational and dramatic intervention from heaven. A writer has wisely said,

"As I see this matter of guidance, God does not put the right ideas into our heads; but if we are in union with Him, He purifies our minds and motives so that we are able to arrive at the right ideas through the faculties which He has given us."

In order that our mental powers may be at their best, we should avoid making a decision late at night or in the early hours of the morning, or when we are ill or tired. Nor is it ever wise to make a hasty decision; it often happens that with time, many of our problems solve themselves.

God works through ordinary means and He sometimes guides us through other people. When Mildred Cable, the intrepid woman traveler, came to the last oasis before the Gobi desert, she hesitated.

"But other people have crossed and left tracks," said her camel driver. "If I lose them, the camels will find them. At night-time there will be the stars and they cannot mislead us. Have no fear, my lady. Rest your heart. There will be a way." Other people can look at our problems objectively and they can help us from their own experience.

Nevertheless, we must take care that we are traveling in God's way. Many have thought themselves to be divinely guided and have become fanatics and despots. If the voices of others or the voice within us counsel what is against God's commandments or the Church's teachings, then they are not the voice of God.

As far as we can, we should try to make decisions that will be unselfish, and we should not be influenced by considerations of what others might think of us. Action can help our deliberations. "Do the duty that lies nearest you; your next duty will then become clearer." Activity relieves the pressure on the mind and helps us to think more clearly. And if a wrong decision has been made, then a new start is better than mere regret. "Mistakes are merely detours on the road to success."

God gives us guidance in response to our prayer, especially prayer that is humble and persevering. Humility implies an openness of mind and a readiness to say, "Thy will be done." Like Bartimaeus, the blind beggar, we must persist with our petition, "Rabboni,... I want to see" (Mk. 10:51). Those who are humble and pray regularly are best disposed to receive God's guidance. St. Augustine says in his *Confessions* that his mother was singularly favored in this way. "She could through some feeling which she could not express in words, discern the difference between your revelations and the dreams of her own spirit."

Finally, devotion to God's will must surely be a certain means of securing His guidance. Christ shows us clearly His own life-long submission to the will of His Father. The Apostle Paul said, "Christ did not please himself" (Rom. 15:3). Our Lord declared,

> "Doing the will of him who sent me
> and bringing his work to completion
> is my food" (Jn. 4:34).

Sometimes it can be agonizingly difficult to make a decision and act upon it, but no human anguish can ever compare with the mysterious agony of mind when Christ prayed in Gethsemani, "Father,...not my will but yours be done" (Lk. 22:42).

There are different ways in which we can say, "Thy will be done." Either we say it in bitter resentment, or in weary resignation, or in loving trust and joyful willingness. May we always have a trustful acceptance of God's will even in the small happenings of life. Thus when we come to the crossroads of an important choice and our way is still uncertain, even after we have pondered and prayed, we shall go forward with complete trust. If this is irrational, then every little child in the world is irrational. All children are perplexed by life. They are always asking questions, and often they are not old enough to understand the answers given them. But the child of a good father understands his love and trustingly puts its hand in his and has no doubts or fears.

Perhaps God, our Father, sometimes leaves us in perplexity so that we may have greater trust in Him. It is only then that He can do most for us and through us.

"He drew me out of the pit of destruction,...
He set my feet upon a crag" (Ps. 40:3).
"No evil shall befall you,
nor shall affliction come near your tent,
For to his angels he has given command about you,
that they guard you in all your ways" (Ps. 91:10-11).

A Happy Sermon

It was a dark December day of cold drizzle. An official from the State Department of Education was inspecting a Catholic school. He was a member of a strict observance sect, and his unsmiling demeanor contrasted with the cheerfulness of the little nun principal. As he was leaving she said to him,

"Come now, we need cheering up on such a miserable day! Let me get you a nice cup of tea."

The man frowned his disapproval. "Sister," he said, "we are not meant to be happy."

Many people associate goodness with gloom, and virtue with dolefulness. To them religion is a negative thing, consisting solely of depressing prohibitions and the renouncement of even innocent joys and pleasures. It is not surprising that religious people are looked upon sometimes as kill-joys.

We ourselves may not be priggish and sanctimonious, but perhaps there is a little of the Puritan in us because we are just a little afraid that God does not intend us to be happy and enjoy life. The sufferings we experience make us think that this world is nothing but a vale of tears and that it would be naive and unrealistic to think otherwise.

But this is not real Christianity. The true Christian refuses to be dismayed by suffering and steadfastly believes that we are meant by God to be happy. St. Paul speaks of "the God who provides us richly with all things for our use" (1 Tm. 6:17).

A producer, rehearsing the British actress Dame Sybil Thorndike for her role in the play *St. Joan of Arc,* said to her, "Don't say the word 'God' in the way unbelievers use it! Say it happily. It is a joyous word."

The happiness of a virtuous life is stressed in the Sermon on the Mount. Described as the most cheerful sermon ever preached, this sermon of our Savior has happiness as its theme throughout.

Scholars point out that in the original Greek and Hebrew, the beatitudes are so worded as to indicate that they are not promises of future happiness, but declarations or exclamations about a present happiness. "Happy" or "O the bliss" or "O the blessedness" are the more correct renderings. It is of course understood that this happiness will reach full completion and perfection in the life after death, but for the Christian, it has already begun and can be experienced in this present life on earth.

What is this happiness or blessedness? Our Lord spoke Aramaic, but the Gospel writers translate into Greek the word He used for happiness by the word "makarios." To the Greek this referred to a bliss that was possessed only by the gods who were truly "hoi makarioi," the Blessed Ones. In the New Testament God Himself is described by this word.

If this is the happiness about which Christ spoke in the Sermon on the Mount, then it follows that Christian happiness is nothing less than a share in God's own life and bliss. It is a happiness that is within us and is independent of outward circumstances. "The reign of God is already in your midst" (Lk. 17:21).

The beatitudes are concerned with the mental attitudes and the inner dispositions of the individual person. They can be divided into two groups. Each group corresponds to a fundamental need we all possess.

We may experience a restless dissatisfaction with life. Voltaire called life a bad joke. We may feel something is missing, or we may be tired and bored because life seems purposeless, or because it has not come up to our expectations. We may be disappointed because we have made a mistake and missed certain opportunities.

"How blest are the poor in spirit...they who hunger and thirst for holiness...the sorrowing..." (Mt. 5:3, 6, 4). The beatitudes are a complete reversal of all worldly standards. "My kingdom does not belong to this world" (Jn. 18:36). The beatitudes seem to point to happiness in the wrong things, but if we examine them more closely, we shall see that this is the only way to *real* happiness.

Christ is obviously not advocating poverty, nor is He praising those who are "poor-spirited." He says there is a special kind of happiness for those who realize their spiritual need, for those who know that material things such as wealth, fame, comfort and almost everything else in the visible world are insufficient, for those who are aware of their own helplessness and who put their trust in God.

Because of their utter destitution, such people have come to depend on God so completely that their dependence has brought them a sense of freedom and security which nothing else could have done.

> "Peace is my farewell to you,
> my peace is my gift to you;
> I do not give it to you as the world gives peace"
> (Jn. 15:27).

Happy indeed are those people who have become quite independent of the changing fortunes of life because of their absolute dependence on God! The truth has made them free of all anxiety and doubt.

Those who hunger and thirst after holiness will have a worthwhile purpose in life. They will not be bored or cynical. No one ever reaches the height of success he wants to reach. The true artist is never satisfied. Christianity is not complacency or idleness. "You must be made perfect as your heavenly Father is perfect" (Mt. 5:48).

Those who mourn are people who really care. They know the blessedness there is in sorrow for sin and in compassion for the sufferings of others. They are the opposite of those whose attitude is one of indifference: "So what? I cannot help it."

The second group of beatitudes proclaims the bliss of a special way of life. Life is precious and fleeting and we need to know how to get the most from it, how it is meant to be lived.

The happiness which Christ describes in the second group of beatitudes is the happiness of His own life on earth. To live in patience and humility, to live in purity and unselfishness, and to live as an instrument of peace and atonement is to experience the height of bliss because it is to live in, with and through Christ. These are the qualities of our Lord Himself, and to practice them in imitation of Him and for love of Him is to share in His life and happiness. Christ tells His disciples:

"I am the vine, you are the branches.
He who lives in me and I in him,
will produce abundantly,
for apart from me you can do nothing" (Jn. 15:5).

The teachings of the Sermon on the Mount are so powerful that if they were acted upon by mankind, our society would be completely transformed.

The beatitudes are only possible to those who know Christ and are united to Him. Christianity is not just a philosophy; it is a life that must be lived. And Christianity is Christ.

Our Lord said, "Come back and follow me" (Mt. 19:21). "Learn from me" (Mt. 11:29). "Live on in me..." (Jn. 15:4). Thousands upon thousands of sermons are preached every Sunday throughout the world, but people are not greatly affected by them and even the best of sermons can be forgotten in time. This will not happen with the important Sermon on the Mount if we keep Christ in our thoughts. Deeds speak louder than words and example is more effective than rules and directives.

I'd rather see a sermon than hear one any day,
I'd sooner one should walk with me than just
point the way.

Christ is the Word Incarnate; He reveals God to us. The Sermon on the Mount is a sermon about Himself. We shall remember it if we remember Him. We shall often think of Him as poor in spirit, obedient to the will of His Father. We shall frequently look upon Him and see His humility, meekness, compassion and purity of heart. And then like all good sermons, the Sermon on the Mount will perhaps set us preaching to ourselves, leading to our resolve to imitate Him in our daily life.

Our Speech Reveals Us

There is a fable about Aesop, the Greek slave who lived before the time of Christ and who is renowned for his many wise fables. He was seated by the roadside near Athens one day when a stranger approached and asked him, "What sort of people live in Athens?"

"Tell me," said Aesop, "where you come from and what kind of people live there." Frowning, the stranger replied, "I come from Argos and the people there are liars, thieves and quarrelsome."

"I am sorry to tell you this," said Aesop, "but you will find the people of Athens much the same."

Later, another stranger appeared and asked the same question, but when Aesop inquired where he came from, the stranger's face lit up with pleasure. "I come from Argos where everyone is kind and friendly and I am sorry to have left them." Aesop nodded his approval. "My friend," he said, "I am glad to tell you that you will find the people of Athens much the same."

One man condemns and another praises, and the great difference between them lies not in the place or people, but in the men themselves. Wherever they went, their words would sow discontent and discord or contentment and harmony.

We all need to reflect sometimes on the great power for good or evil our words may have. Unfortunately, nothing is so indicative of human frailty than the widespread misuse of the power of speech. It is impossible to estimate the harm done by malicious talk, by unkind, angry and slanderous words.

"My own temperament," wrote Pope John, "inclines me towards being agreeable and ready to appreciate the good side of people and things, rather than to criticize and pronounce harsh judgments.... Any kind of distrust or discourtesy shown to anyone, especially to those who are humble, poor or socially inferior, every destructive or thoughtless criticism, makes me writhe with pain."

Christ adopted a stern attitude towards all sins of the tongue. He denounced hypocrisy.

"These people pay me lip service,
but their heart is far from me" (Mk. 7:6).

He gave a solemn warning: "By your words you will be acquitted, and by your words you will be condemned" (Mt. 12:37). He went even further: He declared that on the day of judgment, men and women will have to give an account of every idle word they have spoken. What did He mean? Must we refrain from ordinary conversation and from harmless remarks and pleasantries?

This is certainly not what our Lord meant. To understand Him, we must remember that Christ was always more concerned about the inwardness of sin—the thoughts, motives and intentions. "From the mind stem evil designs—murder, adulterous conduct, fornication, stealing, false witness, blasphemy. These are the things that make a man impure" (Mt. 15:19-20). The sinfulness of idle words does not lie in their thoughtlessness, but in the fact that they are spontaneous and thus reveal what is in the mind and heart. Unintentionally, and often without our realizing it, idle words slip out, bringing into the open the evil that hides within us.

A hostess left a group of guests and walked across the room to an elderly lady who had just arrived. The hostess welcomed her with a radiant smile, "I am delighted to see you. It is so kind of you to have come to my party." But the elderly lady could lip-read and, on entering the room, she had seen the hostess saying,

"Please excuse me. I must speak to that tiresome, boring old woman. I had to invite her, but I was hoping she would decline my invitation." These were the idle words, the words that slipped out, the words that revealed the unkindness within.

"Each man speaks from his heart's abundance" (Lk. 6:45). Our boastful and selfish words reveal our inborn pride; our broken promises show our untrustworthiness; our love of gossip discloses a hidden streak of malice and anger; abusive words show our lack of self-control. Our speech betrays us, and our idle words are like the lazy spiral of smoke on the mountain that indicates the hidden menace of the volcano.

One of the apostles was quiet-spoken and reticent. He was James, and he wrote a letter in which he dwells upon the importance of our words. "It is the same with ships," he writes, "however large they are, and despite the fact that they are driven by fierce winds, they are directed by very small rudders on whatever course the steersman's impulse may select. The tongue is something like that. It is a small member, yet it makes great pretensions.

"See how tiny the spark is that sets a huge forest ablaze! The tongue is such a flame. Every form of life, four-footed or winged, crawling or swimming, can be tamed, and has been tamed, by mankind; the tongue no man can tame. We use it to say, 'Praised be the Lord and Father'; then we use it to curse men, though they are made in the likeness of God. Blessing and curse come out of the same mouth. This ought not to be, my brothers! Does a spring gush forth fresh water and foul from the same outlet?" (Jas. 3:4-6, 7-8, 9-11)

As an old man, Tagore, the great Indian poet and philosopher, often used to recall with tears a priest who had spoken kindly to him when he was a child. But another teacher once said sarcastically to a boy, "Your parents will one day regret that you were their son." That boy made a great success of his life, but the cruel words that had cast a shadow over his youth always rankled in his memory. We have the choice of helping or harming others by our words.

People are indignant if they are denied the right of freedom of speech, but they sometimes overlook the duty to use this right with responsible control. We need to be on our guard and practice restraint in our speech. For our guidance, there are three helpful questions we can ask ourselves on certain occasions:

Is it true? "Nothing is opened by mistake more than the mouth." Often we can be deceived by our personal prejudices and dislikes. Disraeli said, "It is much easier to be critical than correct." Even the "experts" are often wrong.

Some years ago a letter appeared in one of the English newspapers: "Sir, wishing for an expert opinion on a portrait with an indistinct signature, I have had three opinions. One of our best portrait experts pronounced it beautiful and in his opinion, Dutch. A London dealer said it was definitely Italian of the seventeenth century, but not a very good work.

An artist who judges paintings in London declared it to be a portrait of a Shakespearian actress of the late eighteenth century. He also said that an opinion given years ago about it must have been given by a madman." "Expert" opinions certainly can be contradictory!

It is always better to reserve our judgments until we know the whole truth and nothing but the truth, and perhaps by then we shall be more tolerant.

Is it kind? Many good people often display a "holier-than-thou" attitude, and their self-righteousness has unpleasant, and unchristian consequences. A little girl is supposed to have prayed, "Lord, make bad people good, and good people kind." Nothing livens up a flagging conversation so much as the words, "Don't tell anyone, but...." Byron made the shrewd observation:

"Man must serve his time to every trade
Save censure; critics are ready-made."

Remembrance of our own frailties should make us more kindly disposed to overlook the faults of others. "Let the man among you who has no sin be the first to cast a stone at her" (Jn. 8:7).

Finally, *is it necessary?* Doubtless there are occasions when we may be obliged to speak of other people's failings so as to reprove and correct, or perhaps to prevent harm being done to the innocent, but we must always observe charity.

While on a train, Cardinal Gasquet noticed two schoolboys mimicking him as he recited his Breviary. When he had finished and closed his book, he entered into conversation with them. They told him they were returning to school after the summer vacation and they mentioned the name of a famous school.

"Surely not!" the Cardinal exclaimed. "I knew many men from there, but they would never have forgotten they were gentlemen and mimicked an old man saying his prayers." The boys apologized, and the three chatted away like old friends.

However, more often than not, there is no necessity to discuss the weaknesses and shortcomings of others. Merely to relay spicy pieces of gossip is despicable and cowardly. Shakespeare puts it bluntly, "He who steals my purse steals trash, but he who filches from me my good name takes all I have."

During World War II, notices posted in bus and railway depots and wherever people were likely to gather bore the warning: "Careless talk costs lives." This is just as true in times of peace.

We have all known people who have become addicted to lies, slander and malicious talk, but we have also known some who were sincere and never spoke badly of anyone. In each case, the difference in talk reflected a difference in thought. Sins come from within us.

"Sow a thought and you reap an act; sow an act and you reap a habit; sow a habit and you reap a character; sow a character and you reap a destiny." Our words will acquit or condemn us.

Thor Heyerdahl and five other men (all Norwegians except one Swede) went on the wonderful Kon-tiki expedition. They drifted for over three months in all sorts of trying weather and circumstances, on a specially-made raft, all the way from Peru to an island near Tahiti. Afterwards the leader was asked if there were any quarrels or jealousies among them. He replied that he had realized it would be one of the greatest dangers the expedition would have to face. So they had confronted it at the outset.

They had agreed that if they felt like saying anything unpleasant, they should keep silent; that if any one of them failed, the others should remain silent. It worked and they ended the expedition better friends than ever, even though they had lived together on a space no bigger than a carpet. But all of us are together on a kind of raft in this life. May we try to behave like those remarkable men!

The words of Christ show the perfection of His character. No evil or harmful word ever passed His lips. Indeed people were amazed at the way He spoke. They marveled at His sincerity, wisdom and authority. "All who were present spoke favorably of him; they marveled at the appealing discourse which came from his lips" (Lk. 4:22). The better we come to know our Lord, the nearer we approach Him and live in spirit with Him, the more we too will always speak with sincerity, understanding and kindness.

God's Servants

St. Paul's character is in many ways puzzling and difficult to understand. He can seem sure of himself, yet he also said that he was the "least of the apostles" because he had persecuted the Church (1 Cor. 15:9). He can appear severe, yet he was tender and affectionate.

A lady once said she did not like St. Paul because she thought he was anti-feminist. This is a sad misjudgment of the saint. St. Paul had many friends. Some of the letters he wrote contained lists of those to whom he sent his personal greetings, and women friends and helpers are included. He could be strong in his condemnation of evils, but he only mildly admonishes two quarreling ladies: "I plead with Evodia just as I do with Syntyche: come to some mutual understanding in the Lord" (Phil. 4:2). After his martyrdom, it was a wealthy Roman matron, Lucina, who claimed his body and gave it burial in her family tomb.

And then there was Phoebe. In his letter to the Romans, St. Paul writes, "I commend to you our sister, Phoebe, who is a deaconess of the church at Cenchreae. Please welcome her in the Lord as saints should. If she needs anything, give it to her, for she herself has been of help to many, including myself" (Rom. 16:1-2). An interesting story lies behind this brief statement.

St. Paul was in Corinth, apparently on his way to Rome and Spain, but some urgent affairs required his presence back in Jerusalem. He had not yet visited Rome, but he must have longed to go to the imperial city; its dangers and opportunities were an irresistible challenge to him.

He was prevented from going to Rome, so instead, he wrote a letter, an important and valuable letter, which begins: "Greetings from Paul, a servant of Christ Jesus.... To all in Rome, beloved of God and called to holiness" (Rom. 1:1, 7). But once the letter was written, how was it to be delivered? This is where Phoebe comes on the scene, because Phoebe was the bearer of St. Paul's letter.

Nothing is known about her, but St. Paul's concern for her would indicate that she was not wealthy. She may have been accustomed to doing lowly tasks. Perils were everywhere, and weeks, perhaps even months, passed by as she trudged along dusty roads and forest trails, clutching the precious roll of manuscript under her cloak. Doubtless she herself made little of her privations—she had a job to do.

Phoebe could never have written the letter. Only St. Paul could have done that. But at least she could deliver it for him. She was happy to serve in any way she could. It was an honor. And St. Paul, too, takes pride in describing himself as a servant: "Paul, a servant of Christ Jesus..." (Rom. 1:1). Both saw themselves as Christ's servants.

Nowadays, subservience or any kind of obedience and submission is eyed with suspicion. The role of a servant is regarded as an affront against human dignity.

There is not the slightest doubt but that authority can be abused. It has often been a power that corrupts. Nevertheless, obedience is necessary, not only because without it there is disorder and chaos, but because it is the remedy for a disease that has caused all our unhappiness—the deification of self. "I will not serve," cried Satan, and humanity has repeated his insolent refusal.

Christ came on earth to put right this disobedience. St. Paul says,

"He emptied himself
and took the form of a slave,
...he humbled himself,
obedient by accepting even death,
death on a cross!" (Phil. 2:7, 8)

He came as the "suffering servant," fulfilling the prophet Isaiah's prediction, a prophecy which the Jews had never understood. Christ said, "The Son of Man has not come to be served but to serve..." (Mk. 10:45). His whole life was completely dedicated to serving His Father and mankind,

"...I am not seeking my own will
but the will of him who sent me" (Jn. 5:30).

"I am in your midst as the one who serves you" (Lk. 22:27).

Servants, both good and bad, figure in many of our Lord's parables—servants who are needed and who are given responsibilities. At the Last Supper, when Christ washes the feet of His astonished and shocked apostles, He tells them that this is to be their role:

"What I just did was to give you an example:
as I have done, so you must do.

...no slave is greater than his master" (Jn. 13: 15-16).

Throughout history God has used servants. Strictly speaking, He does not need any human assistance, but He has so ordained it that He depends on our aid and cooperation. So He needed the prophets and leaders of the Old Law; He needed our Lady and St. Joseph, St. Paul, the apostles and Phoebe, and the saints and martyrs. The Pope calls himself "Servant of the servants of God."

Properly adjusted people do not find that serving others is repugnant or irksome. "Can I help you?" we sometimes say, and the strange thing is that in helping others we help ourselves. Our nature is such that we find fulfillment and satisfaction in the humble service of others.

We should never think that perhaps if we had been given more talents or if we had been better circumstanced in life, we might have served God better. However restricted our activities and sphere of influence may be, we are always God's dedicated servants, ministering to Him in the way He wants.

Sitting up in bed and gasping for breath, St. Bernadette joked, "I am at my job." Cardinal Newman's words should banish any misgivings or doubts we may have: "God has created me to do Him some definite service; He has committed some work to me that He has not committed to another. I have my mission—though I may never know it in this life....

"I have a part in a great work; I am a link in a chain, a bond of connection between persons. He has not created me for naught. I shall do good, I shall do His work; I shall be an angel of peace, a preacher of truth in my own place, while not intending it, if I do but keep His commandments and serve Him in my calling. Therefore I will trust Him.

"Whatever and wherever I am, I can never be thrown away. If I am in sickness, my sickness may serve Him; in perplexity, my perplexity may serve Him; if I am in sorrow, my sorrow may serve Him. My sickness or perplexity or sorrow may be necessary causes of some great end which is quite beyond me. He does nothing in vain; He may prolong my life, He may shorten it; He knows what He is about. He may take away my friends, He may throw me among strangers; He may make me feel desolate, make my spirits sink, hide the future from me—still He knows what He is about...."

God makes no distinction of persons; often He chooses the weak and the foolish to confound the strong and the wise. We are all His servants, whether we are first or second strings in His orchestra, whether we are a Paul or a Phoebe. We must always be grateful for this.

"We thank you for counting us worthy to stand in your presence and serve you." Let us humbly pray that we may always remain in His service.

"It's Only Me"

This is the space age in more ways than one. Not only has space exploration seemed to dwarf our tiny planet into insignificance, but everything around us tends to be on a large scale. There is almost a cult of bigness. Sprawling, overcrowded towns, huge firms, mammoth industrial units and colossal deals involving billions of dollars have become accepted commonplaces. We do more and we do things "bigger" than ever before...and not always in the best interest of man. In the past half-century, more people have been terrorized, enslaved and murdered than in any other previous period of history.

Serious-minded men and women are bewildered and apprehensive, and many young people are rebellious because they are frustrated. They feel that individuals no longer matter. They resent being turned into automatons of some vast communal ant-hill.

Long ago the psalmist praised God because He was the Lover of the individual as well as the Ruler of outer space.

"He heals the brokenhearted
 and binds up their wounds.
He tells the number of the stars;
 he calls each by name" (Ps. 147:3-4).

Christ came on earth to proclaim God's love of every human being. Although He was the Savior of all mankind, He lived among, sought out, and called by name individual people. Like a good shepherd, He knew each of His flock and was ready to leave the ninety-nine to go in search of the one lost, straying sheep. He told of the Father's care being such that the very hairs of our head are numbered.

Our Lord emphasized the importance of small things. He spoke of the widow's mite, the grain of mustard seed, the cup of water, and of the harm that could be done by a single word. He warned that not an iota, not a dot, would pass from the law until all was accomplished.

In life it is the small things that are often of great importance and worth. We marvel at the human brain, so small in size, yet containing several thousand million cells; we stand in awe before the wonder of a single cell. The microscope reveals as many mysterious marvels as the telescope.

"The world will never starve for want of wonders," declared Chesterton, "but only for want of wonder." Nowadays, only the spectacular and the sensational can stir our jaded sense of wonder; we take for granted the minor miracles.

In the affairs of life, big events often have small beginnings. The Russian revolution is said to have started when a woman in a bread-line threw a stone through the window of a store. A New York District Attorney said, "Fully half the cases in our criminal courts originate in little things—bar-room bravado, domestic wrangling, an insulting remark. These are the little things that lead to assault and murder."

A man on Scott's expedition to the South Pole had to live six months cooped up with a companion in the terrible cold and darkness. He confessed that at night he felt like violently attacking him for sucking a piece of candy in bed before going to sleep!

A writer has said, "Trifles make up the happiness or misery of life." In this cosmic and apocalyptic age we should not scorn the small and the commonplace. Our lives may seem very ordinary, our achievements insignificant and our sphere of influence restricted, but one of the mysteries of life is the way a smile or a word or a single small act can sometimes have an unforeseen effect.

One morning many years ago, in the little village of Kirriemuir, Scotland, a woman was reading a letter she had just received. Her face became white and drawn because the letter contained bad news. Her son David, away at school, was ill and the mother must hurry if she was to see him alive. Quickly she made her preparations in a strained, silent way that alarmed her other children, especially James Matthew, who was only six.

They went with her to the railroad depot. While she was getting the ticket, her husband went to the telegraph office. Soon he returned. "It's too late," he said. "David has gone." They all turned and went back home.

Day after day, the mother lay in a darkened room, a look on her face that frightened little James Matthew. His father said to him, "James, you must comfort her." Timidly he approached the dark, silent room and stood gazing towards the bed. His mother whispered, "Is that you?"

James thought she meant his brother David and he answered, "No, it's not him. It's only me."

The droll, sad words touched a hidden spring in the mother's heart, and she wept the healing tears. It was the beginning of a close and wonderful understanding between the Scottish playwright James Matthew Barrie and his mother.

Someone has said that God loves little saints. We may be far from being even little saints, but He who has told us to learn of Him because He is meek and lowly of heart will never despise the small offerings that are made to Him from humble and contrite hearts. The little act of self-denial, the small unselfishness, the ready acceptance of some pain or disappointment, the prompt turning from temptation, the kindly spoken word, the smile of encouragement when we feel more like crying, the suppressed hasty criticism or unkind remark and the fervent ejaculatory prayer—all these may be trifles, but they can be tremendous trifles. They are our way of saying,

"Here I am, dear Lord. It's no great or even little saint who is trying to serve You. It's only me." God heeds the singer more than the song; He regards the giver more than the gift.

Does It Matter?

In his renowned story of the Good Samaritan, Christ may have been describing a real incident. The road from Jerusalem to Jericho had a notorious reputation for bandits. If it was a true story, scholars give us an explanation of what may have passed through the priest's mind when he came upon the robbers' victim. According to Jewish law, had the priest so much as touched the wounded man, he would have become legally "unclean," and if the man had been dead, the priest would have been unable to practice any of his priestly functions for twenty-four hours, after having performed lengthy purifying ceremonies.

It is easy for us to see that the priest had gotten his priorities all wrong. What he thought was important did not really matter. However great the inconvenience to himself or others, even if he had had to spend a week in cleansing ceremonies, he should never have walked past a dying man.

This is not to say that love of our neighbor and good works should take the place of love of God. There is that occasion in the Gospels when Christ was at the home of Mary and Martha and the latter complained fretfully because she was left with all the work to do, while her sister merely conversed with their guest. Our Lord gently rebuked her,

"Martha, Martha, you are anxious and upset about many things; one thing only is required" (Lk. 10:41). It was another instance of misplaced priorities.

The things that matter and the things that do not matter! In his autobiography, *Chronicles of a Wasted Time,* Malcolm Muggeridge, a former editor of the British humor magazine, *Punch,* declared, "As I look back, it is amazing how much that seemed important at the time now seems negligible—ambitions, passions and the rest."

The things that matter and the things that do not matter! When we look back over our lives, we can now see the differences very clearly. If only we had known earlier, how much needless suffering and anxiety we might have been spared!

There were occasions when we almost made ourselves sick with worry and fear about things that never happened. We wasted a dreadful amount of time and energy on useless things, and neglected good and worthwhile matters because of our laziness and selfishness. Then there were the many times when our feelings were hurt by some trivial misunderstanding, or when we were angered by some slight or disappointment. If only we had been more reasonable and not made mountains out of molehills!

"Life is too short to be little," remarked Disraeli. How true, and yet we are often small-minded and behave like spoiled children. Many good causes have perished, many friendships have soured and many marriages have been wrecked because some small disagreement, dislike or jealousy was allowed to fester and grow. The delightful musical partnership of the two Victorians, Gilbert and Sullivan, was broken because of a quarrel about a carpet.

A divorce court judge declared, "Trivialities are at the bottom of most marital unhappiness." Some years ago the newspapers reported the divorce of a couple who had not spoken to each other for several years; it had all begun because the wife wished to invite to supper friends whom the husband disliked. They had quarreled, and years of built-up hostility and wounded pride had followed.

The things that matter and the things that do not matter! Obviously, we cannot expect to get through life without having some trials and hardships. We must be prepared to face unpleasant and even evil things. We must do what we can to alter them. We cannot be indifferent or permissive simply to avoid distressing ourselves. Unfortunately, there are many wrongs, sufferings and evils about which we can do little or nothing.

"God grant me the serenity to accept the things I cannot change, courage to change the things I can, and wisdom to know the difference."

It is not always easy to know the difference. Much of Christ's teaching was centered upon the essentials and the nonessentials of life. There were those who had no religion and who were deeply engrossed in the material things of the world. To them He said, "What profit would a man show if he were to gain the whole world and destroy himself in the process?" (Mt. 16:26) But the Jewish religion itself had become encumbered with a great mass of petty restrictions; Christ swept them aside and proclaimed the principal commandments, love of God and love of neighbor. Modern life can be very complicated and so we too need this great simplification.

We can never love and trust God too much. St. Paul says, "We know that God makes all things work together for the good of those who have been called according to his decree" (Rom. 8:28). Juliana of Norwich, a medieval mystic, wrote a book entitled *Revelations of Divine Love.* In it she declared,

"On one occasion the good Lord said, 'Everything is going to be all right.... You will see for yourself that every sort of thing will be all right.' He wants us to know that not only does He care for great and noble things, but equally for small, lowly and simple things as well. We see deeds done that are so evil and injuries inflicted that are so great that it seems impossible for any good to come out of them. We are unable to know the supreme wisdom, might and goodness that belong to the Blessed Trinity. It is as if He were saying: Be careful now to believe and trust, and in the end you will see it all in its fullness and joy."

Whatever trials and misfortunes may threaten us, we shall never let ourselves be overwhelmed by fears or worries because of our strong belief and trust in God's love. We can never love and trust Him too much. It is His love that matters above everything else in life.

The great St. Teresa was another mystic. She was born of a noble Castilian family and reformed the Carmelite order. For all her holiness and her visions, she was practical and down-to-earth. There is one short sentence in her writings that sounds especially modern and to the point. It is not profound, but it is worth remembering: "You can never be too good-tempered."

It often happens in life that we face the major problems and disasters bravely, but it is the little frictions of everyday life that upset us so easily—the small blows to our self-esteem, the little contradictions, the pinpricks that irritate, and the petty grievances that swarm about us like troublesome flies. If we are earnestly trying to be Christlike, we shall not waste a single moment brooding over the faults of others nor resenting any harm they may do us. These things do not really matter, and we shall not let them distress us. It is more important that we seek to be like our Lord, patient, forgiving and good-tempered, and loving our neighbor for His sake always.

Towards the end of his long life, Pope John wrote, "I repeat once more that what matters most in this life is our blessed Lord Jesus Christ, His holy Church, and the truth and goodness of His Gospel. Our goodness must be meek and kind, hard-working and patient, unconquerable and victorious."

Journey into Light

There is a realistic note about the Gospel incident of the Magi, or astrologers, which should satisfy the modern craze for realism. They were wise men from the East, and the Orient with its mystery cults is famous for its baffling, secretive ways. Perhaps they were astrologer priest-kings of some Persian religion.

The star, or whatever celestial phenomenon it was that they followed, may have been something entirely miraculous, or it could have been a comet, or the conjunction of two planets. They interpreted it to mean that something of importance had taken place—the birth of a king. The Jewish expectation of the Messiah was widely known at this time.

There is even some realism about their gifts in spite of the symbolic meaning usually attached to them. They were valuable and perhaps they were of practical help to the Holy Family in its early struggles, especially when it became a refugee family in Egypt. Later on, Christ was to express His indebtedness to strangers.

Judaism was God's preparation for the Son of God's coming on earth but, in a lesser degree, so were other nations—the Greek world with its advanced culture and philosophy, and the Roman way of life with its law and order. Nowhere does God leave Himself without some witness and He is the Lover of all mankind. His own may not receive Him, but Christ is the "light of the world" and God "gives light to every man" (Jn. 1:9).

The Epiphany incident is not without some meaning for each of us. Our life is a journey—a journey from mystery to mystery. G. K. Chesterton said that modern man has not only lost his way in life, but he has lost the map. Seneca wrote long ago, "When a man does not know what harbor he is making for, no wind is the right wind."

What is so mysterious about human life? Animals do not find life a mystery, so why should we? To the animal, life is merely survival, a matter of obtaining sufficient food and comfort. Is it any different for us? Secular humanists answer, "No." They are obsessed by the thought of survival, and they are very worried people. They worry that there may not be enough food, enough freedom and enough living room.

Secular humanism is the most subtle enemy of religion. It professes half the Christian Faith—the love of humanity, but it is a love that excludes God.

The central Christian belief of Christianity is not survival, but God. Of what use is survival unless it means God and survival after death? Men and women are not satisfied with bread alone; they have longings and loves that reach out beyond the stars. Our journey through life is mysterious because our destiny is mysterious. Our journey's end is supernatural; it is no other than God Himself. The saints were obsessed by this thought of "God alone." Everything else was secondary to them, and they were not worried, even though they were deeply concerned about their fellow men.

In our imagination, we perhaps tend to romanticize the journey of the astrologers, but we must keep to our realism. For all their wisdom, they must have had some doubts and misgivings about their interpretation of the star. Perhaps they had some regrets, too, reproaching themselves for their folly. It was wintertime and their way led through strange, hostile territory.

The star disappeared when they had almost reached the end of their journey. Not only were they perplexed, but they must have felt fear and misgiving in the Kremlin-like court of the half-Jewish tyrant, King Herod. They did not hesitate or turn back, however. All the urgency and single-mindedness of their purpose is expressed in the words that announced their arrival in Jerusalem and revealed their great obsession. "Where is the newborn king of the Jews? We observed his star at its rising and have come to pay him homage" (Mt. 2:2). When they continued on their way, the star reappeared. Soon they reached their destination and "they were overjoyed..." (Mt. 2:10).

For us Christians, life is a journey into the light. We do not grope our way in the gloom of fear and bewilderment. We know the reason why we are here and the purpose of our existence. We do not rely on the light of reason alone, because we have the light of faith, the light of Christ's teaching and the light of the good example of others.

Yet this does not prevent life from having its trials and difficulties. "Life is for real." Often it is just dull and ordinary, but there are times when we have to contend with irksome tasks and exasperating people; we have worries and sickness, doubts and fears; we get weary and fainthearted.

And then sometimes the light seems to go out altogether. We have some great trial, a shock, a serious illness, a bereavement. Prayer and the spiritual life are dry and unreal; God seems remote and even non-existent. The psalmist described it as our entering the dark valley; St. John of the Cross called it "the dark night of the soul."

Like the Magi we must keep resolutely on through the darkness. There must be no turning aside or going back. When we feel alone in the darkness and when our strength seems to fail us, argument and logic are of little help to us. All we can do is to keep on praying for God's continuing help.

There is a sad little sentence in St. Paul's letter to his young friend Timothy: "Do your best to join me soon, for Demas, enamored of the present world, has left me and gone to Thessalonica" (2 Tm. 4:9). The affectionate Paul must have had a heavy heart as he wrote those words.

We know nothing about Demas. His name had been coupled with that of St. Luke, the beloved physician, so perhaps he was prominent and widely known in the Church, and had helped to brighten the apostle's imprisonment. Perhaps he had great ability and had been a zealous worker, but had later changed. Hardships and discouragement, duties and fastings, unsympathetic listeners and carping critics, wearying journeys and boring companions—the light that had once burned so brightly must have dimmed, flickered a few times and finally gone out. There is no blame or excuse, just the sorry little admission: "For Demas, enamored of the present world, has left me" (2 Tm. 4:9).

We are all potential defectors; none of us is immune from the temptation to turn back and give up. But we have a supernatural destiny, and we must use the supernatural means of regular prayer and reception of the sacraments to attain it. And perhaps we should pray more often for the grace of final perseverance and for all who are tempted to discouragement and despair.

Standing Before the Door

A young woman in a small town in Germany had advertized a pianoforte recital. She claimed to have been a pupil of Liszt, but this was not true. The day before the recital, the young pianist was horrified to learn that the famous musician himself was visiting the town! She knew her deception would now be discovered, and her hopes of making a career ended.

Rather than leave the place, she decided to tell her story to the composer. In great distress she sobbed out her confession, explaining that she was alone in the world and was trying to earn a living. Liszt looked at her kindly.

"You have done wrong," he said, "but we all make mistakes and I can see you are ashamed and sorry. Now let me hear you play." The young woman obeyed, timidly at first, but later gaining confidence.

Liszt corrected her in a few places and then said, "I have instructed you a little, so you are now my pupil. You may go ahead with your concert and you can announce that the last number will be played, not by the pupil, but by the master."

It is always gratifying when someone is fair in their judgment and treatment of a fellow human being. Many of the world's famous trials illustrate man's blunted sense of justice. The trials of St. Joan of Arc, St. Thomas More, and Mary, Queen of Scots, are but a few of the trials that were unfair, illegal travesties of justice.

We are as ready to condemn as we are unwilling to accept blame. Henry VIII of England was idly playing dice with Anne Boleyn when messengers brought the news of St. Thomas More's execution. "You—you are the cause of that man's death!" Henry suddenly flung at her, and then strode from the room.

We are always concerned that justice should at least *appear* to have been done. The first Queen Elizabeth authorized the death-warrant of her cousin Mary, Queen of Scots, but after Mary had been safely disposed of, Elizabeth wrote to Mary's son James to say that it was a lamentable accident which had happened contrary to her wishes.

Everyone believes in justice and judgment. We all feel very strongly that those who do evil should not be allowed to get away without having some punishment and that those who do good should be rewarded. One man lives like an animal and another like St. Francis of Assisi—will it all be the same in the end? Our reason refuses to believe that this would be right.

But there are many crimes that go unpunished, terrible injustices that linger on for years. And how can the full extent of a wrongdoing be adequately assessed in one lifetime? "The evil that men do lives after them, the good is oft interred with their bones." The consequences of a lie, an act of cruelty, or a book written against faith or morals are sometimes wounds that never heal.

We believe that at the end of every life there is a judgment, a final reckoning, a scrutiny of that person's life and character. It is then that full justice will be done. If this were not so, it would mean that God does not know everything, or that He does not care, and either is quite unthinkable.

The Judgment is an essential part of Christ's teaching. In His parables He gives many vivid pictures of the Judgment. At His own trial He declared that He Himself will come in power and majesty as the judge of mankind. He often warned of the need to be watchful and ready.

The man who lives as though he will never be judged and delights in his well-stocked barns is called a fool, and in the parable of the virgins those who grew tired of waiting and are unprepared are described as foolish.

The imagery is never exaggerated. "Then the door was barred" (Mt. 25:10). Could there be anything more final and terrible than this picture? There have been many doors in our lives and perhaps we recall them uneasily: the door at which we waited for a dread interview; the door behind which someone we loved lay sick, grieving or dead; the doors of prisons, hospitals, trains, planes and buses—we have stood before them all in apprehension, fear and misery. God grant that His door may never be closed against us!

But it would be wrong to think that our Lord's motive in teaching the Judgment was to instill dread and compel us to serve Him from abject fear alone. On the contrary, He seems to imply that the Judgment should be regarded with a certain relief and joy. "Will not God then do justice to his chosen who call out to him day and night?... I tell you, he will give them swift justice. But when the Son of Man comes, will he find any faith on the earth?" (Lk. 18:7-8)

In the *Te Deum*, the Church's hymn of thanksgiving, is the exultant phrase, "We believe that You will come to be our judge." The early Christians looked with longing for our Lord's second coming. In the acclamation after the consecration in the Mass, we can express our own joyous belief in the ultimate triumph of right over wrong and of justice over every injustice: "Christ has died! Christ is risen! Christ will come again!"

The Scriptures have two little pieces of advice that should sweeten the thought of the Judgment. For most of us, school and college examinations were unpleasant and disquieting. They were necessary, even though their results were not always the most satisfactory way of judging ability and character. Sometimes the one who did brilliantly made no effort, while the one who did poorly had worked diligently. However, a good preparation always lessened the dread of an examination, and this is what the Scriptures recommend:

"If we were to examine ourselves, we would not be falling under judgment..." (1 Cor. 11:31). It is not always easy to take the blame for a fault or a mistake. We dislike blaming ourselves. An official of a world-famous prison said that in his life-long association with criminals, he had never met any who blamed themselves. Adam said, "The woman...gave me fruit from the tree, and so I ate it" (Gn. 3:12), and Eve's excuse was, "The serpent tricked me into it" (Gn. 3:13).

"If we were to examine ourselves..." (1 Cor. 11:31). This is precisely what we do in confession. Perhaps we do not sufficiently realize that the sacrament of Penance is an anticipation of our judgment. The throwing of a stone into a lake gives some indication of what happens in confession. There is a slight sound, a splash and a few ripples; then the calm surface of the lake is restored, but the stone has vanished. The sins which we have confessed and for which we are repentant and have made atonement will never be brought against us at our judgment.

"If you want to avoid judgment, stop passing judgment" (Mt. 7:1). Our own weakness and guilt should make us hesitate to point the finger of scorn and condemnation at others. "Forbear to judge, for we are sinners all," says Shakespeare. One of the most dramatic incidents in the Gospel is that of a woman being dragged before Christ and accused of adultery. Our Lord responded by calmly challenging the unhappy woman's accusers. "Let the man among you who has no sin be the first to cast a stone at her" (Jn. 8:7). One by one the men drifted away and only our Lord remained to judge and pardon. If Christ is so slow to pass judgment, dare we presume to be so hasty and righteous?

Judge not, because we usually see only outward appearances and these are often deceptive. An intelligent young man had needlessly spent twenty years in a mental hospital merely because his father had died when he was a boy and he was thought to have developed aggressive tendencies. Human behavior is complex, unpredictable and even irrational. Who except God can disentangle the maze of emotions, influences and motives that lie at the root of human thinking and conduct?

Judge not, because it is kinder and more tolerant to make allowances and excuses for others. Lincoln used to make excuses for army deserters during the Civil War. "I could never know but what I should be tempted to drop my rifle and run, if I myself were in the line of battle."

"To step aside is human," said the poet Burns. "Gently scan your fellow man." We need to make allowances for others because they may have some secret handicap of temperament, upbringing or environment, some hidden malady or fear. A writer has said, "God makes immense allowances, using His inexhaustible wisdom."

Judge not, so that you will exercise greater humility, patience and charity. You will have peace and better relationships with others, but above all, you will become more Christ-like. To be tolerant in our judgments is not to condone something that is clearly wrong, but it is to imitate our Lord, who hated the sin, yet had pity and pardon for the repentant sinner: "You may go. But from now on avoid this sin" (Jn. 8:11).

The only one who can judge fairly is the One who not only knows what we did but what we tried to do; who knows that we sometimes failed, but also that we sincerely repented of our failure; who knows us even better than we know ourselves.

"He knew them all. He needed no one to give him testimony about human nature. He was well aware of what was in man's heart" (Jn. 2:24-25). And we shall not only be judged fairly by Jesus, but we shall be judged with infinite love and compassion.

Today Is Shaping Tomorrow

An elderly, fiery dissenter was disgusted with present-day preachers. He described them as "mild-mannered men, who in a mild manner, try to persuade mild-mannered people to be more mild-mannered." In the past, people listened spellbound to lurid, hell-fire sermons, but in our modern sophisticated age, they get their entertainment from films of horror and violence, and hell seems old-fashioned and outdated.

But even if a polite silence on this subject may have blanketed the once thunderous pulpits, the law of retribution still operates and we cannot disregard it. Nothing in life is so plain to see as the inflexible law of retribution. Carlyle wrote, "A lie returns to its starting point though it takes a century to reach it." Retribution is one of nature's fixed laws; it is the law of cause and effect. The word is derived from the Latin *retribuo*—"I give back." It is the reaping of what has been sown. As we sometimes say, "The pigeons come home to roost."

Some years ago, the London Times reported a strange case of crime in a German town. A lady one day found a basket on her doorstep. Inside it was a pigeon and a letter warning her that if she did not fasten a certain sum of money to a clip on the bird's leg, her house would be burned down.

She informed the police, who acted quickly. They tied a streamer of ribbon to the pigeon's neck and when the bird was released, a plane followed it to a neighboring town. When it flew down, the pilot radioed its position and a police car drove up just as two men were unfastening the telltale ribbon. They denied that the pigeon belonged to them. "It just flew down into our yard."

The police said they would make a test; the pigeon was taken to another distant spot and again it came back. The men finally confessed their guilt and were arrested.

Sin is like that; it always comes back. The law of retribution never fails to operate. Sin may give us what we want, but it also gives us what we don't want. Of its very nature sin is evil and ultimately the evil must take effect. Emerson said, "The specific stripes may follow late upon the offense, but they follow because they accompany it. Crime and punishment grow out of the same stem. We cannot do wrong, without suffering wrong." "The wages of sin," says St. Paul, "is death" (Rom. 6:23).

In the Bible, David committed adultery and tried to hide his sin by murder, but he had to pay a terrible price. Gehazi, the prophet Elisha's servant coveted a cloak of fine cloth and sinned to get it; he succeeded, but he also got a cloak of leprosy. Judas got the agreed sum of money, but he could hardly bear even to touch it. History has countless examples of the law of retribution. Many of the scourges afflicting modern society are retribution for crimes committed. One cannot but dread the future effects of present-day godless education and legalized murder of the helpless unborn.

One can try to overlook almost anything in Scripture if he so chooses, but it is very hard to overlook the fact that Scripture clearly teaches a doctrine of a real hell. Nothing is more definite and clear.

All the passages relating to hell come from the lips of our Lord Himself; in each instance He is most explicit, as if He wished to guard against being misunderstood. St. Matthew's Gospel is very vivid: "Every tree that does not bear good fruit is cut down and thrown into the fire" (Mt. 7:19). "The chaff he will burn in unquenchable fire" (Mt. 3:12). "The gate that leads to damnation is wide, the road is clear" (Mt. 7:13). Even in the Gospel of the gentle St. Luke we read: "Fear him who has power to cast into Gehenna after he has killed" (Lk. 12:5).

If there is no hell, no possibility of losing God for all eternity, why should salvation be the main theme of the Scriptures and why should Christ have used such words as loss and destruction? Perhaps the most frightening description of the fate of the unrepentant sinner is in our Lord's words to His apostles, "You are the salt of the earth. But what if salt goes flat? How can you restore its flavor? Then it is good for nothing but to be thrown out and trampled underfoot" (Mt. 5:13).

The full implication of these words is lost upon us, but among the Palestinian inhabitants it was a well-known fact that the salt of their country—rock salt gathered from dried-up lakes and from the localities at the south end of the Dead Sea—becomes insipid and useless when exposed to the rain and sun or in contact with the ground. Earth and other impurities are sometimes gathered with it so that it effloresces and turns to dust—but not to fruitful soil.

In addition to being worthless in itself, this impure and corrupted salt actually destroys all fertility wherever it is thrown. There is no place for it about the house, yard or garden, and it must be carefully swept up and thrown into the street, there to be trodden underfoot.

People today pride themselves on being realists. We certainly ought to give some thought to our responsibilities and to the inexorable law of retribution. What is happening to us now is in part the result of what we did or did not do yesterday, or perhaps long years ago. For instance, we may be enjoying some comfort or happiness today because years ago we worked hard and lived prudently; or we may have anxiety and disappointments now because we made mistakes or did wrong in the past and the consequences are overtaking us at this moment.

In the same way, today is shaping tomorrow. What we think, plan and do now can make us happy or miserable next week, in ten or twenty years, and after death. Surely it is only being reasonable and realistic to pause and make sure, as far as we can, that our today is shaping a sunny tomorrow, that our present is a preparation for an eternity of life and happiness.

Home

Every journey has its destination, every road has its ending. Rivers find their way to the ocean, ships come into harbor. And nothing is more certain than that our life is terminated by death.

Yet our instinct to live is so strong that while we see death claiming others around us, it is difficult to realize that one day it will be our turn. Sometimes we say with cheery fatalism, "We only die once," and this is true, but once is enough, and death is worthy of serious consideration.

Death is both sad and strange. It is sad because it takes from us those we love. It is a final parting. All partings are sad; the French and the Italians even say, "To part is to die a little." After the death of someone we love, our own life has to go on, but things are never quite the same again.

An unusual radio interview was given in 1970, by Les Carron, the British Trade Unionist who had been a Communist until he was disillusioned by the corruption he found in Communism. The interview took place just two weeks before he died. He knew he had incurable cancer, but his mind was alert and he spoke without emotion. He was asked what his feelings were at the near approach of death.

He said that he was not a religious man and that he felt only great disappointment. He loved his family and home; his work for others had brought him satisfaction and happiness. He had enjoyed travel, talk and good food. He had had a successful career. Now that his full and interesting life was coming to an end, he could only experience the deepest disappointment.

Death is not only sad, but it is strange. It quenches the cheerful flame of life, and nothing seems to remain but an unreal silence, emptiness and remoteness. Death is strange because it seems all wrong that two of life's most precious possessions, love and happiness, should apparently be destroyed.

If indeed death were a complete end to love and happiness, it would be more than a disappointment. It would be a senseless and cruel joke, for it would be like snatching away the cup from a thirsty man when he has taken only a few sips of water. What would be the use of knowing you were going to die if death meant annihilation? We would be better without a mind if it could only tell us that death is oblivion.

But reason rebels at the notion that our life ends like a flame that has been snuffed out. Science declares that nothing is ever completely annihilated; constant change is going on, but there is never annihilation. Nature is always taking steps to avoid this total destruction, and the humble grass seed provides an example of this.

In every handful of grass seed are what are termed "hard" seeds—perhaps only one or two. The usual rule is that when any seed falls into the ground, it dies and then grows. But the few "hard" seeds do not do this. They lie dormant through several seasons, and even years. Then one day they stir and grow. It is nature's way of keeping a reserve on hand. Should there be some exceptional catastrophe so that the usual crop is destroyed, the species will not be annihilated, since once the danger has passed, the "hard" seeds will come up here and there, spreading new life again. Now nature, we know, works under the providence of God.

Christianity teaches that death is the gateway and beginning of a new life. Christianity itself is based upon this teaching because it rests solely upon the resurrection of Christ. One of the most insidious attacks of Modernist theology is its denial of the reality of Christ's resurrection. "If Christ has not been raised,...your faith is empty," says St. Paul (1 Cor. 15:14).

Our Lord's death seemed senseless and cruel, but His resurrection was a glorious conquest of death. He taught clearly that all His disciples would share in that same triumph, that our life's journey, like His, will lead beyond the rim of earth's horizon.

"I am the resurrection and the life:
whoever believes in me,
though he should die, will come to life;
and whoever is alive and believes in me
will never die" (Jn. 11:25-26).

The real test of our Christian orthodoxy is our belief that our bodies will be raised and joined again to our souls at the resurrection. "The Father raises the dead and grants life, so the Son grants life..." (Jn. 5:21). Christ said,

"No need for you to be surprised at this,
for an hour is coming
in which all those in their tombs
shall hear his voice and come forth.

Those who have done right shall rise to live;
the evildoers shall rise to be damned" (Jn. 5:28-29).

The life after death seems mysterious and unreal, but our Lord Himself has left us a description that is more realistic than harps, golden crowns and thrones. He often spoke of our dwelling and abiding with Him; and the night before He died, He said,

"Do not let your hearts be troubled.
Have faith in God
and faith in me.
In my Father's house there are many dwelling places" (Jn. 14:1-2).

St. Paul said, "We have a dwelling provided for us by God, a dwelling in the heavens, not made by hands but to last forever" (2 Cor. 5:1). And St. John in his vision of heaven said, "Then I saw new heavens and a new earth.... I heard a loud voice from the throne cry out: 'This is God's dwelling among men'" (Rev. 21:1, 3).

To those who have known a good home this description of the life after death may help to take away some of its strangeness. Our "dwelling" or "home" is so much a part of us and gives us such a sense of security and "belonging" that most dying people ask to be brought home for burial. Jacob, growing old in Egypt, expressed the yearning to be laid to rest with his kindred, "Have me taken out of Egypt and buried in their [my ancestors'] burial place" (Gn. 47:30).

But home is not just roof and walls alone. It is the people who live in it that transform a building into a home. Home means security, happiness and love; it is the place where we can relax and be ourselves. It sometimes happens that we can be far from home, living among strangers, but because of their kindness we make what is called a "second home." Yet always deep in our affections is our true home in our native land.

Heaven is our true home. Here on earth we are strangers in an alien land. Here, there is no security and no rest. Endings and partings constantly mar our happiness; the wear and tear of life can corrode our companionships. In our home in heaven everything will be very different. "There shall be no more death or mourning, crying out or pain, for the former world has passed away" (Rev. 21:4).

Our home in heaven will not be strange or unreal to us because we will not have gone among strangers! We shall have the companionship of those who are already familiar and close to us—our Lord, our Blessed Mother, our parents, relatives, and the countless friends and acquaintances who people heaven.

Thoughts such as these may help to take away some of the sadness and strangeness of death, especially if they are coupled with prayers for perseverance to the end. Cardinal Newman prayed that when the busy world became hushed and the fever of life was over, he might be given a safe lodging and peace at the last.

"O my Lord and my Savior, support me in that hour in the strong arms of Your sacraments and by the fresh fragrance of Your consolations. Let the absolving words be said over me and the holy oil sign and seal me, and Your own body be my food and Your blood my sprinkling. Let my sweet mother Mary breathe on me, my angel whisper peace to me and the glorious saints smile on me; that in them all and through them all, I may receive the gift of perseverance and die as I desire to live: in Your faith, in Your Church, in Your service and in Your love."

Just before he died, St. Thomas More, the English martyr, who had a great love for his home and family, wrote to his daughter from his prison in the Tower of London: "Pray for me, and I shall pray for you and all your friends that we may merrily meet in heaven."

In his "Spiritual Testament," Pope John wrote, "Oh what a fine band of souls awaits us and prays for us! I think of them all the time. To remember them in prayer gives me courage and joy, in the confident hope of joining them in the everlasting glory of heaven!"

May we live in faith and love, in the firm hope that no matter how long the night and dark, the dawn will surely come, ushering in the eternal day.

Daughters of St. Paul

In Massachusetts
50 St. Paul's Avenue, Boston, Mass. 02130
172 Tremont Street, Boston, Mass. 02111
In New York
78 Fort Place, Staten Island, N.Y. 10301
625 East 187th Street, Bronx, N.Y. 10458
525 Main Street, Buffalo, N.Y. 14203
In Connecticut
202 Fairfield Avenue, Bridgeport, Conn. 06603
In Ohio
2105 Ontario St. (at Prospect Ave.), Cleveland, Ohio 44115
E. Eighth Street, Cincinnati, Ohio 45202
In Pennsylvania
1127 South Broad Street, Philadelphia, Pa. 19147
In Florida
2700 Biscayne Blvd., Miami, Florida 33137
In Louisiana
4403 Veterans Memorial Blvd., Metairie,
New Orleans, La. 70002
86 Bolton Avenue, Alexandria, La. 71301
In Missouri
1001 Pine Street (at North 10th), St. Louis, Mo. 63101
In Texas
114 East Main Plaza, San Antonio, Texas 78205
In California
1570 Fifth Avenue, San Diego, Calif. 92101
278 17th Street, Oakland, Calif. 94612
46 Geary Street, San Francisco, Calif. 94108
In Canada
3022 Dufferin Street, Toronto 395, Ontario, Canada
In England
57, Kensington Church Street, London W. 8, England
In Australia
58, Abbotsford Rd., Homebush, N.S.W., Sydney 2140,
Australia